Negotiation at Work

Maximize Your Team's Skills with 60 High-Impact Activities

Negotiation at Work

Maximize Your Team's Skills with 60 High-Impact Activities

Ira G. Asherman

AMACOM

New York • Atlanta • Brussels • Chicago • Mexico City • San Francisco
Shanghai • Tokyo • Toronto • Washington, D.C.

This publication is designed to provide accurate and authoritative information in regard to the subject matter covered. It is sold with the understanding that the publisher is not engaged in rendering legal, accounting, or other professional service. If legal advice or other expert assistance is required, the services of a competent professional person should be sought.

Library of Congress Cataloging-in-Publication Data

Asherman, Ira.
    Negotiation at work : maximize your team's skills with 60 high-impact
activities / Ira G. Asherman. — 1st ed.
        p.   cm.
    ISBN 978-0-8144-3190-0
    1. Negotiation—Study and teaching.   I. Title.
BF637.N4A85   2012
658.4′052—dc23

                                                    2011046256

Portions of this book were published as *50+ Activities to Teach Negotiation*, by Ira G. Asherman and *50 Activities for Sales Training* by Philip Faris, both published by HRD Press, Inc.

Beach A & B scenarios on pages 225 and 227 are adapted from *Negotiating Rationally* by Max H. Bazerman and Margaret Nealie, Free Press, 1992, p. 32. The Boundary Role worksheet on pg. 257 is adapted from *Interorganizational Negotiation and Accountability: An Examination of Adams' Paradox* by Cynthia S. Fobian, National Institute for Dispute Resolution, 1987. The worksheet for The Adams Paradox on pg. 261; adapted from "The Structure and Dynamics of Behavior in Organizational Boundary Roles" by J. S. Adams, *Handbook of Industrial and Organizational Psychology*, M.E. Dunnette, ed., Rand McNally, 1976.

About AMA

American Management Association (www.amanet.org) is a world leader in talent development, advancing the skills of individuals to drive business success. Our mission is to support the goals of individuals and organizations through a complete range of products and services, including classroom and virtual seminars, webcasts, webinars, podcasts, conferences, corporate and government solutions, business books, and research. AMA's approach to improving performance combines experiential learning—learning through doing—with opportunities for ongoing professional growth at every step of one's career journey.

Printing number
10 9 8 7 6 5 4 3 2 1

CONTENTS

PDF files for the handouts and PowerPoint files for the overhead slides
are available to purchasers of this book at:
www.amacombooks.org/go/NegotiationWork

HANDOUTS AND OVERHEADS

www.amacombooks.org/go/NegotiationWork

OVERHEADS

INTRODUCTION

Negotiation is an interactive activity that requires a variety of skills. It is not limited to the process of making concessions, offers, and counter offers. It requires self-awareness, good questioning, listening, and conflict resolution skills, as well as an ability to understand the needs and interests of others. We have therefore included exercises that cover all of these issues.

THE ORGANIZATION OF THIS BOOK
The exercises in this book are grouped by topic and presented in the following chapters.

Opening Activities (3 activities)
These activities are designed to open a negotiation program or to serve as pre-work materials. As pre-work materials, they begin the process of orientation before people arrive in the workshop.

Planning (2 activities)
These activities are designed to help people understand all the issues they need to consider when planning for a negotiation.

Creative Thinking (2 activities)
We find that many people are limited to yesterday's answers and are not creative in finding new ways to approach problems. These two activities are designed to address that concern.

Negotiation Skills (4 activities)
These activities are designed to look at the behaviors critical to being a successful negotiator.

Negotiating Styles (3 activities)
These activities are designed to help look at how we deal with conflict. They are best used in conjunction with negotiating styles or conflict resolution feedback surveys.

Assertiveness (3 activities)
These exercises are closely related to the styles section and are designed to show the relationship between assertive behavior and successful negotiation.

Questioning Techniques (3 activities)
Critical for all negotiators is the skill of questioning. These three exercises are designed to help participants practice this skill.

Ranking Exercises (3 exercises)
These three exercises stimulate discussion on issues specific to negotiation.

Surveys (2 activities)

These surveys are designed to help people evaluate their current skills. They can also be used to initiate a program. The surveys are self-scoring.

Case Studies (12 cases)

These cases address a variety of issues unique to negotiation. They can be used to support a range of learning objectives.

Negotiation Transcripts (4 transcripts)

These scripts are taken from several negotiation audios and videos we developed. We have also used them, without the videos, as case studies. They are valuable, since each explores the actual dialogue of a negotiation. Tapes of the transcripts are also available.

General Exercises (4 activities)

These exercises can be used in a variety of places in a program. Some are designed to support specific exercises in your program.

Needs and Interests (2 activities)

These activities are designed to help look at one's needs and interests, as well as those of the other party.

Difficult People (1 activity)

This exercise is designed to help participants practice dealing with difficult people.

Boundary Roles (3 activities)

These three activities are best when used with people who serve in a boundary role function. They explore the boundary role concept and its implications.

Sales Negotiation (10 activities)

These materials are designed specifically to present issues unique to the sales function.

THE ORGANIZATION OF THE ACTIVITIES

Each activity in this book is presented in two sections: the first comprises the activity's basic instructions; the second provides the PDF files for participant handouts. The instructions section includes such components as:

- Objectives: The goals of the activity.
- Time: The amount of time needed to conduct the activity.
- Group Size: The optimal number of participants for the activity.
- Materials and Equipment: The things needed to complete the activity.
- Trainer's Notes: Important issues for the trainer's attention.
- Procedure: The steps to follow in conducting the activity.

Lecture notes are also included in the activities that warrant them. The handouts vary according to the exercise they facilitate. Most of the activities are straightforward, although some require special treatment if they are to work. In such cases, information is provided in the Trainer's Notes.

In conclusion, we wish you the best negotiation sessions with these activities. We trust that they will work as well for you as they have worked for us.

FEEDBACK

We are always interested in feedback on these exercises and how they have worked for you. In addition, if you have exercises you have used that you are willing to allow Asherman Associates to include in future books, please let us know. We can be reached in New York City at 212-243-0782.

VIDEOS

The scripts on pages 23 and 203 are available on videotape for $34.95 each. The two Ted and Sandy scripts are currently available on audiotape for $10.95. Both can be ordered from Asherman Associates, Inc., 210 West 19th Street, New York, NY 10011 (Fax 212-243-1375).

ACKNOWLEDGMENTS

A special word of thanks is in order to Sandy Asherman, who reviewed the entire manuscript and made a significant contribution to the final product.

Thanks also to our administrative assistant, Yahaira Norris, who patiently typed and retyped the book's many drafts.

I would also like to thank Glenn Parker, my roommate in graduate school, long time associate, and very special friend, who not only encouraged me to undertake this book, but provided continued guidance and support throughout the process.

—Ira G. Asherman

SYMBOLS

 HANDOUT

 CASE STUDY

 OVERHEAD

I. Opening Activities

A Current Negotiation

Objectives:	To get participants thinking about the program prior to their attendance
	To provide participants with a current negotiation that they can work on during the program
Time:	45 minutes, spread throughout the program
Group Size:	Small groups should ideally be two people, but three or four can work.
Trainer's Notes:	This material should be distributed approximately two weeks prior to the program. This activity can be used for both sales and nonsales groups.
Procedure:	During the program, you should stop several times to let the participants discuss the pre-work with a partner of their choice. They should meet with the same person each time. Question 7 should be discussed near the very end of the program.
	We conduct a brief discussion at the conclusion of the program to determine if the participants have any insights into the problem.
	If you choose to conduct a discussion at the conclusion, do the following:
Step I	*Allow 15 minutes for participants to discuss Question 7 with their partners.* Encourage them to be as specific as possible.
	Note: Listen in on the discussions. If any appear particularly interesting, ask if group members would share their plan with the larger group.
Step II	Ask for volunteers to discuss their plan.
	Ask the following:
	• How does this differ from what you have previously done?
	• Why have you decided on these steps?
	• Will this plan be difficult to implement?
Step III	Thank people for volunteering.

PRE-WORK: A Current Negotiation

Directions:

To make the upcoming negotiation workshop as relevant and specific to your needs as possible, please describe a negotiation you are currently conducting or one you will conduct in the future. If possible, select a negotiation that you expect will be difficult and one with which you would like some help. Please bring this form to the workshop.

This material will be discussed during the workshop, but not collected.

Individual's Name: _____

Department: _____

Company Name *(if appropriate)*: _____

1. What are the issues being negotiated?

2. What do you want from the other party? What are your objectives?

3. What do you think he or she wants from you? What are their Objectives?

4. What were the results of prior meetings on this issue?

5. How would you describe your relationship with this person?

6. What obstacles (if any) do you anticipate in reaching a satisfactory solution?

7. Based on what you learned during this program, what steps should you now take? Be specific.

Expectations

Objectives: To have participants identify what they want to learn in the program

Time: 35 minutes

Group Size: Small groups should be no more than four people. Pairs will also work well.

Materials: Bring extra copies of the worksheets to the class.

Trainer's Notes: This material should be distributed approximately one week prior to the program. During the program opening, it should be used as a vehicle to discuss participants' expectations for the session. The first page can be used by itself at the beginning of the program.

Procedure:

Step I At the beginning of the program, ask participants to meet with others at their table to discuss the pre-work. Emphasize that they should focus on the situations in which they negotiate, as well as their expectations for the program. Responses to the other questions should be shared within the group. Allow 10 minutes.

Step II *Reporting Back*

Ask each group to report on their negotiation situations and their expectations for the workshop.

After participants give their reports, ask them how many with negotiations are with people they have done business with before. Most negotiations will be with people they have dealt with previously and will deal with again. We usually point out that this type of negotiation requires special skills because the relationship is critical. This is not a traditional win-lose negotiation such as takes place in a flea market or with a car dealer. *Allow 10 minutes.*

Step III After listing the types of negotiations, ask people to report on their expectations for the program.

Discuss their expectations with emphasis on which items you will cover and when, and which items will not be included in the program. For those items that will not be included, suggest options for how they can be addressed. For example, books or meeting with you after class, etc. *Allow 15 minutes.*

PRE-WORK: Expectations

Directions:

To ensure that the upcoming negotiation program meets your needs and concerns, please answer the following questions:

1. Think about situations in which you negotiate, both in your job and your personal life. Write down every example you can think of.

Business	Personal

2. What do you see as your strengths as a negotiator? In what ways do you think you need to improve?

Strengths	Improvement Opportunities

3. What would you like to learn about negotiation? What would make this program useful for you?

Everyone Negotiates

Objectives:	To help participants see the universal nature of negotiation
	To provide a framework for the negotiation program
Time:	15 minutes
Trainer's Notes:	It is our experience that most people think of negotiation as something conducted by diplomats and labor leaders, and only very occasionally by themselves. This exercise will help them see how frequently they negotiate. It is similar to the prior exercise and *should be used if you do not send out pre-work.*

Procedure:

Step I   Ask the participants to complete the attached worksheet. Allow 5 minutes.

Step II   *Reporting Back*
Ask participants to report back on their negotiations; post the results.

Step III   After the list is completed, ask the participants "to think about the people involved in these negotiations." Then ask, "Are these people you will see once, or are they people who will come back into your life?"

Most participants will indicate that they will come back repeatedly.

Point out that the program is designed to look at negotiations where you know you will see the other parties again. These negotiations are special and require special skills. They are not typical win-lose negotiations.

Also point out how frequently we negotiate, both on the job and in our personal life.

Step IV   Ask participants to share their expectations for the program.

Post the results.

Point out any expectations the program will not meet.

WORKSHEET: Everyone Negotiates

Directions:

On this worksheet, list situations in which you negotiate in both your business and personal life.

Business	Personal

What would you like to learn about negotiation? What would make this program useful for you?

II. Planning

Negotiation Planning

Objectives: To practice the planning process

Time: 60 minutes

Group Size: Small groups should be three or four people. There is usually too much discussion in larger groups, and people have difficulty getting focused.

Trainer's Notes: This exercise can be done with any role-play. We have included two role-plays which are not related to each other. The roles are used as a vehicle for this exercise. The ideal would be to use one that relates to the occupational background of the participants.

Procedure: Conduct a brief lecture on planning. Cover the points below. Allow 10 minutes.

Step I
- *Issues*—Why are we meeting? What topics do we need to cover?

- *Objectives*—Both our own and the other party's. It is also important that we rate our objectives. Are some more important than others?

- *Needs and Interests*—These are the underlying issues that may be motivating the other person and giving rise to what he or she says.

- *Concessions*—What am I prepared to give up in an effort to move the process along?

- *Settlement Options*—What do I see as a possible deal that would work for both of us? It is important to come up with more than one option and to identify your least acceptable result.

Step II Hand out one copy of the Negotation Planning Worksheet to each participant. Point out that effective planning requires that we look at ourselves as well as the other person.

Step III Divide the participants into small groups, and hand out copies of one of the attached role-plays. Everyone gets the same role-play. The objective for each group is to develop a plan for the negotiation assigned to it. Ask each group to put its report on flip-chart paper for presentation. *Allow 20 minutes.*

Step IV Each group makes its presentation. Point out the similarities and differences among the groups and how one's definition of the objectives leads logically to possible settlement options. If there are differences, it is important to point out that in negotiation there is no one right answer or plan. Also highlight the value of working with others in the planning. *Allow 30 minutes.*

WORKSHEET: Negotiation Planning

	ME	OTHER PARTY
ISSUES Why are we meeting		
OBJECTIVES What we want to achieve		
NEEDS AND INTERESTS Intangibles		
POTENTIAL CONCESSIONS Can be given up		
SETTLEMENT OPTIONS Possible answers		

ROLE-PLAY: The Alpha Project—Chris

You were very excited when your boss asked you to chair the Alpha Project team 18 months ago. You have never chaired a team before and feel that this could have a positive impact on your career. The project involves the implementation of a new software program that could have real value to the company. Mike is one of the team members, and you have worked with him on several projects during the past several years. You generally find him responsive and easy to work with. However, he missed last month's meeting and just this morning called your secretary to say that he won't be available for next week's meeting. This is not typical. You're not happy with Mike's level of participation; you feel that he is ignoring his responsibilities to the team. There are a number of reasons why you feel this way.

- In the last six months, Mike has missed three meetings and hasn't sent a replacement. Prior to that time, he was at every meeting.

- Because of Mike's unavailability for meetings, the team was late with its monthly status reports on two separate occasions.

- Several weeks ago, you had to make major revisions in Mike's section of the quarterly report because what he turned in was inadequate. If he had submitted a draft to you as everyone else did, the problem could have been easily solved. This is not typical of Mike.

- Several times in the past three months, you called ad-hoc meetings and weren't able to reach Mike. It would have been helpful if he'd been available, since these were issues he was knowledgeable about.

You can't afford to let Mike sacrifice your reputation. His poor performance is affecting the team. What makes the problem worse is that several team members have commented to you about Mike's performance and the effect it is having on the team. As one member said, "We need management's input, and if Mike can't participate, then we need someone who can."

You have spoken with your boss about the problem. She agreed that the problem is important, but suggested that you try to work it out with Mike before she gets involved.

You really don't want your boss to intervene since it would indicate that you can't handle the tough problems. She did make it very clear that she is concerned and wants you to get the problem resolved—but how this is done is up to you. Both of you see the Alpha Project as critical.

You have asked to meet with Mike in an effort to let him know how you feel and to see if these problems can be resolved and put behind you. You have not talked to Mike about your concerns before today.

ROLE-PLAY: Engineering—Dana Kent

You have consistently liked your current employer's Purchasing people; they are always ready to expedite your requests. Their system works like a charm. If you need a particular piece of equipment or engineering/construction services, you first meet with a vendor to work out the details and then send the paperwork to the appropriate buyer. Unless there is some problem, the equipment/service always shows up when it's supposed to.

This procedure works very well for you; you've been in the business quite some time and know what you need. You don't need much, if any, help from Purchasing. You have the budget, you know the vendors, and your boss has given you the authority to make the needed purchases. Compared to your previous company, this is a real pleasure. Where you formerly worked, the Purchasing people were always eager to become involved "up front," working with you to get the "best deal." As a result, you didn't always get exactly what you wanted and the process took much longer. In addition, you doubt that they got a better price. Your experience with those Purchasing people was that they were too concerned with price.

Last week, Lee Larson of Purchasing, called asking for a meeting. When you asked about what, Lee said he wanted to discuss how they could work with you in the coming fiscal year. You hate to even think about what this might mean! You have several major projects coming up in the next year and have already begun discussions with several vendors. The biggest project will be a manufacturing GMP upgrade, which will require engineering and construction management services. This project will cost upward of $30 million. You are not sure how much Lee knows about the upcoming projects, but you have no doubt he's heard something through the grapevine.

Right now, nothing is an emergency, but you want to make a decision about the engineering firm in several weeks. This shouldn't present a problem. While there are several good engineering and construction firms, you would prefer to deal with Vax Engineering, a relatively small firm that specializes in GMP upgrades. You've worked with Vax in the past and its performance has been excellent. Equally important is the company's Project Manager—Janet Vincent. You and she have been talking about this project for at least three months, even before the appropriation request was written. You know and like Janet; service is her key. You have a large conference coming up in several weeks, and you can't afford to be bothered with the details of getting the project started. You know that Janet is willing and able to take care of all that for you in your absence.

And, while you haven't begun any discussion on the other projects, you have ideas about the companies you want to work with. Allowing Purchasing to get involved only promises to complicate matters and upset relationships you already have.

As you think about this meeting, you'd really like to keep Lee out of the process. You like the current arrangements: you make decisions and Lee takes care of the paperwork. Maybe you'll be lucky and that's all he wants to talk about—especially since you anticipate an additional $20 million worth of expenditures during the rest of the fiscal year.

You mentioned Lee's call to your boss, and he said that you should do whatever makes you feel comfortable.

You are about to meet with Lee. Take the next several minutes to prepare for the meeting.

Behind the Lines

Objectives:	To evaluate a sales representative's planning To identify the elements of effective sales planning
Time:	Step I—20 minutes Step II—25 minutes
Group Size:	Four people in each of the small groups.
Materials:	Copies of the case for each person. You should bring extra copies.
Trainer's Notes:	This case works best as part of a program for sales representatives. It is a relatively long case and should be used as an assignment between class sessions. It can also be used as a pre-work assignment. Asherman Associates has a video of the meeting between Karen and Paul, which is available for purchase.
Procedure:	
Step I	Divide participants into small groups. Ask each group to discuss the questions at the conclusion of the case.
Step II	*Reporting Back* • Ask each group to give its report. • Invite groups to critique one another's reports.
Answers: **Question 1**	*What do you think of Karen's plan?* Her plan is not bad, but her lack of attention to the commodity items raises some concern. It looks as if she is prepared to give up too quickly.
Question 2	*How well do you think she prepared for Universal's price hike?* She worked well with M.D.s but probably should have given Paul more time, not just reports. She should have met with him.
Question 3	*How would you suggest Karen begin?* She should clarify where Paul is coming from, the pressure he is under, what his needs are, and, if possible, what he is getting from Whitney. She should try to get past positions to underlying needs and interests.

Question 4   *How should Karen utilize her concessions?*
Carefully. She should not put them on the table until she is clear about Paul's concerns and how the concessions can address those concerns.

Question 5   *Should she have done anything differently?*
Yes. Invest some effort to determine what Whitney was doing in her territory and spend more time with Paul.

CASE: Behind the Lines

BACKGROUND

It came as a rude shock when Paul Delano, purchasing manager for Blair Hospital, called to tell sales representative Karen Nape that he might not renew Blair's procurement contract with Universal Hospital Supply.

Karen had been selling Universal's products to Blair Hospital's Coronary Care Unit for three years and, during the past several months, had been working to ensure a smooth renewal of the contract. In fact, she'd been working doubly hard in anticipation of price increases on some of Universal's products. For instance, Karen has worked closely with Blair's Cardiac Catheter Lab's internal Product Evaluation Committee (PEC) to test her products and to verify their quality. She met with all of the physicians and the nurses during the past year; several of them more than once. If the end-users requested her products—especially if they validated the new, improved features that justified Universal's price increases—Karen figured she would be less subject to challenge on price. And the PEC *had* strongly endorsed the new items. In addition, since Paul Delano had the final say, Karen tried to reinforce her case by sending him reports highlighting the end-users' comments on her customer service and on the cost advantage of Universal's superior quality. For example, because Universal's catheters rarely failed, so only one catheter might be needed instead of two or more of a competitor's less expensive catheters.

Until Delano called, Karen had been congratulating herself on having done everything necessary to secure her hold on Blair's business. However, she was generally aware of factors that could have threatened that hold. For instance, she knew that Paul had been under some pressure from the hospital's administration to control expenses. In fact, all hospitals were coming under pressure to cut costs. And she knew of at least one competitor—Whitney Surgical Products—that was making an aggressive price discount play for business throughout her territory. Karen had heard from several people that Whitney was offering at least a 7.5 percent discount and would go higher if the company thought the business was a real possibility. In fact, these were the very factors that had prompted her to make her case so carefully over the past few months. And all had seemed to be going well—she had received nothing but positive feedback from Paul Delano until now. At his request, and in preparation for an upcoming meeting that she had requested with him, Karen sent him a listing of her sales to the hospital in each product category for the past year. Her catheter sales amounted to just under $60,000, equally divided between the A and B catheters, and syringes amounted to approximately $17,000. The two were usually sold as a package. Blair was not only her largest account, but its cardiology staff was highly respected and she needed them in her corner. This was not business she could afford to lose.

In addition, Karen sold a variety of other laboratory supplies to Blair. They came to about $18,000 per year but were all low-margin items that did not add much to her salary or the firm's bottom line. Still they were not something she wanted to give up.

During his phone call, Delano had strongly hinted that he had a competitive proposal. His interests might be genuine—in which case, she would have a serious fight on her hands to preserve her largest account. On the other hand, he might be feigning interest in the competition simply to get a better deal. Delano was a tough businessman and a tough negotiator. His first concern was always the hospital. Paul was proud of the fact that he was a member of the hospital's management council; he felt it said a great deal about how he was viewed. Karen faced a ticklish challenge: going all out to preserve Universal's preeminent position as supplier to Blair's Coronary Unit, but doing so without offering lower prices. Consequently she had relatively little room to maneuver.

Based on what Karen knew, she had reached a point over the past three years where she had just about all of Blair's general catheter business. What she did not have were the specialty items—Whitney's strong suit—which amounted to approximately 30 percent of the hospital's orders. This was an area that Universal was trying to move into, and they had recently developed an approach to producing and marketing a limited number of specialized catheters. In addition, one of the physicians at Blair had tested several specialty catheters and indicated that they worked well. However, no orders were forthcoming.

Whitney also manufactured general purpose catheters and syringes, but they didn't come close to Universal's quality. Whitney didn't have the ability to provide either the volume or the customer service that was required. However, although Whitney's sales force was relatively small, they were now making a real push. Ventura Medical recently had purchased a controlling interest in Whitney and was using its financial resources to expand their product base. They had increased Whitney sales force to make a real push for Universal's general catheter business.

After Delano's call, Karen pulled her Blair file out of the drawer and reviewed the situation in detail. During the following week Karen met with her boss to review options. They decided to do everything possible to hold their current level of catheter and syringe business with Blair, since those were high-profit items critical to the company's success. They clearly did not want to come down on price—getting into a price war with Whitney was a losing proposition. Ventura had deep pockets and was known to buy market share at the expense of short-term profits. In order to counter Whitney/Ventura's push into the market for general purpose catheters and syringes, Universal developed a multifaceted plan that included the following:

- A "Just-in-Time" delivery system, with Universal warehousing the goods

- Free delivery on the above

- Price protection for two years, with a two-year commitment at no less than current volume

- Buy back of old stock, in the form of credit toward new goods

- Funds to help advertise the Coronary Care Unit

- Staff-education support or partial sponsorship of educational conferences

The first three items were no problem, and Karen's boss gave her complete authority to use them as needed. None cost the company very much since they regularly were provided to a number of clients. Karen's boss told her to be careful with the buy-back; although they both knew it could close the sale, it would be at a great expense and set a precedent Universal was not anxious to establish. Karen was told to use this option only if she felt the sale would be lost without it, or if Whitney was about to take a major share of their business. In either event she was to call her boss first. Help with the hospital's advertising was a totally new concept and not something that had been used anywhere in the company. Karen's territory had been selected as one of its three pilot test areas. Management preferred that this option be used only after a sale had been made; however, everyone agreed that Karen could use it if specific guidelines were worked out. Support for staff education was also new but could be used if the guidelines were clear. The company didn't want to pay for family trips or first-class tickets to some distant city.

In addition to all of the above concessions, Karen wanted to emphasize the long history and the quality of Universal's service and products. As she indicated to her boss, her feeling was that if they could get close to Whitney's price, the service/quality issue could make the difference. In addition, Karen felt she had a good working relationship with Delano. There was a high level of trust between them that was clearly working for her.

OBJECTIVE

Karen's objective for this meeting was to preserve the catheter and syringe business. She was not overly concerned with the commodity business, but didn't want to lose it. Delano had made it clear during their phone conversation that he wanted to discuss only the A and B catheters. As he said, "That contract is now up for renegotiation. Any other business can be discussed at a later date." Although Karen had hoped to open the door to Universal's specialty items and tie the two issues together, she felt she had little choice in the matter.

QUESTIONS

1. What do you think of Karen's plan?

2. How well do you think she prepared for Universal's price hike?

3. How would you suggest Karen begin?

4. How should Karen utilize her concessions?

5. Should she have done anything differently?

III. Creative Thinking

The Moffett Picture

Objectives:	To practice creative thinking
Time:	15 minutes
Group Size:	Size is not an issue with this exercise.
Materials:	Copies of the case and rules for brainstorming for each person.
Trainer's Notes:	There is an actual answer to this case. Roosevelt's campaign manager wrote Moffett. He didn't tell him that the material was already printed, but rather asked Moffett how much he would pay to have the campaign use the picture. Moffett offered $250, which was accepted. When you share this with the group, it will also raise questions about ethics in negotiation. Many will be uncomfortable with the solution.
	This example was drawn from *The Manager as Negotiator* by David A. Lax and James K. Sebenius (1987, pp. 117–118). Further resources on creative thinking can be found in the Appendix.
Procedure:	
Step I	Distribute the case.
	Allow several minutes for participants to read it.
Step II	Open the floor for discussion. Ask the group to brainstorm a list of responses about how its members would solve this case. Many will offer to pay Moffett something or ask if he would consider a donation of the picture. The actual solution is given very infrequently. Allow 10 minutes.
Step III	When the group is finished, share the actual answer. Ask for their reactions to what the campaign manager did. Allow 5 minutes.
Step IV	Summarize and close. If you have conducted programs on creative thinking, you should deliver a brief lecture at this point.
Alternative:	This activity can also be used as an ethics activity. If you do, focus on the behavior of Roosevelt's campaign manager.

CASE: The Moffett Picture

In 1912 Teddy Roosevelt was running for President of the United States. To reinforce his platform, he planned to distribute a pamphlet, on the cover of which was his picture. Three million copies of the brochure had been printed. Just before they were to be distributed, a campaign worker noticed a small line on each photograph that read "Moffett Studios—Chicago." Moffett held the copyright, and no one had obtained permission to use the photo. Unauthorized use could cost the campaign as much as $3 million. The campaign needed the pamphlet but did not have $3 million.

What would you do?

The Unsold Glasses

Objectives:	To illustrate the process of creative thinking
Time:	20 minutes
Group Size:	15–20
Materials:	Copies of the problem for each person. Flip-chart and markers. Rules on brainstorming for each person.
Trainer's Notes:	This exercise can be done with any object. It would be an ideal exercise for a sales negotiation program if you can bring something your company sells.

Procedure:

Step I　Tell the group members that they will now look at the process of creative thinking. Distribute copies of the following handout and ask the group to read it. *Allow 5 minutes.*

Step II　Before you begin, remind the group of the rules of brainstorming. Do a brief lecture on brainstorming.

Step III　Ask the group to brainstorm solutions. Post the responses on a flip-chart. Encourage group members to list as many examples as possible. *Allow 15 minutes.*

Step IV　Help the group apply this concept to its own planning and to ways its members might be more creative. Ask them for a situation that they are having difficulty with and go through the brainstorming process.

PROBLEM: The Unsold Glasses

One of your largest accounts has asked you to supply his restaurant chain with 5,000 clear glasses with his company crest on them. The client has 25 restaurants in his chain, with 3 more set to open in the next 6 months. This is a new item for this account and is something you can easily provide. Because of a mistake on a print order for another client, you have 6,000 glasses in inventory.

The big problem is that the glasses you have in stock are not clear, but have a blue tint. Each glass also has a basketball, a baseball, and a football engraved on it. Your boss has told you to figure out a way to get the client to buy the blue-tinted glasses. She does not want to carry the inventory any longer. The glasses have been sitting in the warehouse for six months. They are all packed and ready for shipment and are of higher quality than the ones the client wants.

What would you do?

IV. Negotiation Skills

Behaviors of the Successful Negotiator

Objectives:	To identify the behaviors of the effective negotiator
Time:	45 minutes
Group Size:	Small groups of four to six.
Materials:	Copy of the exercise for each person. Flip-chart, magic markers, tape or push pins, and a flip-chart for each group.
Trainer's Notes:	You can use this activity as a freestanding exercise or combine it with the exercise that follows. We suggest that they be used together and that the directions be combined. These exercises should be used early in the program.

Procedure:

Step I   Ask each group to develop (1) a list of the behaviors of an effective negotiator and (2) a list of behaviors to avoid. *Allow 5 minutes.*

Step II   Distribute the attached worksheet. Divide the group into small groups of four to six people.

Ask each group to develop a list of behaviors for the successful negotiator and to identify any behaviors that should be avoided.

Step III   Ask each small group to develop a composite list and to place its list on flip-chart paper.

Direct them to select the three most important behaviors. ***Allow 10 to 15 minutes.***

Step IV   Debriefing

- Ask each group to report on its list and to highlight the three most important items.

- Ask each group to explain why the three items are most important. *Allow 15 minutes.*

Step V   Summarize the similarities and differences among groups. *Allow 5 minutes.*

WORKSHEET: Behaviors of the Successful Negotiator

Directions:

In the left column below, list the behaviors that, in your opinion, an effective negotiator would utilize. In the right column, list the behaviors an effective negotiator should avoid.

Behaviors to Utilize	Behaviors to Avoid

Self-Evaluation

Objectives:	To evaluate current skills
Time:	25 minutes
Group Size:	Small groups of two or three.
Materials:	Self-evaluation sheet for each person.
Trainer's Notes:	This exercise can stand by itself or be conducted as a follow-up to the previous exercise. We suggest that it be used in conjunction with the previous exercise. Either way, it should be used at the beginning of a program.
Procedure:	

Step I   Distribute the Self-Evaluation Worksheet.

Step II   If you are conducting this exercise in conjunction with the previous one, give the following directions:

"Working individually, use the small-group reports that we just completed and select the items that you believe are most critical to your success. You may add additional items. Once you have selected the items, rate your current behavior and identify what you want to work on during the program." *Allow 10 minutes.*

Step III Have participants meet with one other person to review their lists, obtain feedback, and identify the behaviors they want to work on during the program. *Allow 5 minutes.*

Note: These pairs should become partners for the remainder of the program.

WORKSHEET: Self-Evaluation

Directions:

In the columns below, evaluate your skills as a negotiator. In column 1, enter the most important skills you believe a negotiator should have. Enter these in order of importance, with the first skill being the most crucial to you. We have left room for 10 items, but you can list fewer. In column 2, rate yourself on these skills, using a scale of 1 to 5, with 5 being very effective. Column 3 is for any comments that you may want to make.

1. Very Ineffective   2. Ineffective   3. O.K.   4. Effective   5. Very Effective

This material will not be collected and is only for your personal use.

1 Skills of the Effective Negotiator Ranked in Order of Importance	2 How I Rate Myself	3 Comments
1.	1 ⇐⇐ 3 ⇐⇐ 5	
2.	1 ⇐⇐ 3 ⇐⇐ 5	
3.	1 ⇐⇐ 3 ⇐⇐ 5	
4.	1 ⇐⇐ 3 ⇐⇐ 5	
5.	1 ⇐⇐ 3 ⇐⇐ 5	
6.	1 ⇐⇐ 3 ⇐⇐ 5	
7.	1 ⇐⇐ 3 ⇐⇐ 5	
8.	1 ⇐⇐ 3 ⇐⇐ 5	
9.	1 ⇐⇐ 3 ⇐⇐ 5	
10.	1 ⇐⇐ 3 ⇐⇐ 5	

Cross-Cultural Negotiation

Objectives:	To develop a list of the skills required for the effective cross-cultural negotiator
Time:	40 minutes
Group Size:	Four or five people for the small groups.
Trainer's Notes:	You can use this activity as a freestanding exercise or combine it with the exercise that follows. We suggest that they be used together. These exercises should be used early in the program. If you need additional material on this issue, see *Kiss, Bow, or Shake Hands* by Morrison, Conway and Borden, Ph.D., or contact The David M. Kennedy Center for International Studies at Brigham Young University, 280 HRCB, P.O. Box 24538, Provo, UT 84602.
Procedure:	
Step I	Divide the group into several small groups.
Step II	Give the following directions:
	"You have been appointed by senior management to a committee that will select a team of employees to represent the company at negotiations with our non-U.S. customers.
	"Select a country in which your company is doing work."
	Distribute copies of the the Cross-Cultural Skills Worksheet and ask participants to begin work. Point out to the groups that half are playing themselves, the remaining groups will play the country we will be doing business with.
	Have each group record its list on flip-chart paper. *Allow 15 minutes.*
Step III	Ask each group to present their definition of a successful negotiation and list of skills to place the list on flip-chart paper.
Note:	Pay special attention to the definitions of a successful negotiation, as they frequently differ from culture to culture. Point out these differences and their implications for the negotiators.
Step IV	Explore the similarities and differences in their definition of a successful negotiator and the skills required. Discuss the impact on our ability to negotiate effectively with each other. *Allow 20 minutes.*
Step V	Summarize.

WORKSHEET Number 1: Cross-Cultural Skills

Directions:

Please review the following and record your answer below.

You have been appointed by senior management to a committee that will select a team of employees to represent the company at negotiations with (select a country). How do you define a successful negotiation? What specific skills do you think are necessary to be a good negotiator? In what way are they different from the skills required to negotiate in the United States?

WORKSHEET Number 2: Cross-Cultural Skills

Directions:

Please review the following and record your answer below.

You have been appointed by senior management to represent the company in negotiations with a supplier from another country. How do you define a successful negotiation? What specific skills are necessary to be a good negotiator? In what way are they different from the skills required to negotiate in your own country?

Negotiation at Work: Maximize Your Team's Skills with 60 High-Impact Activities, ©2012 HRD Press.
Published by AMACOM Books, American Management Association, www.amanet.org.

Perceptions and Trust

Objectives:	To illustrate how perceptions of others can have an impact on the negotiation process
Time:	30 minutes
Group Size:	10–20
Materials:	Trust Profile Worksheet for each person.
Trainer's Notes:	If you have time, put participants in small groups before the full group discussion. This exercise works well with Ranking Exercise number 3.
Procedure:	
Step I	Distribute the attached *Trust Exercise* worksheets.
Step II	Direct participants' attention to the Trust Profile section of the worksheet. Give them these directions.
	"In the top left-hand box, write the name of someone you trust a great deal; then fill in the appropriate boxes.
	"When you are finished, go to the top right-hand box and record the name of someone you do not trust; then fill in the appropriate boxes."
Step III	Ask participants to begin work. *Allow 15 minutes.*
Step IV	Lead a discussion about the differences between the two and the potential impact of trust on their negotiations.
	Say, "We now want to take this one more step and look at the items that help build trust."
	Ask the group to think about people they trust. What is it they have done that shows they are people who can be trusted?
	List each item.

Note: Items we have found to be most critical are

- They meet their commitments
- No surprises
- Consistent
- Give people credit
- Admit mistakes
- Admit when they do not know something
- Take responsibility for their actions
- Do not make threats

Step V   Deliver a brief lecture on the impact of trust on negotiation. Include the following points:

- People are more open when they trust each other. When trust is low, people are more circumspect and careful about what they say.

- The more difficult the problem, the more critical is trust.

- You can take a tougher bargaining stance with people you trust and whose word you can most likely believe.

Note: This activity could end after Step V. If you have sufficient time, move on to Step VI.

Step VI   Tell participants to turn to the Action Planning section of the worksheet. Ask them to use it as a framework to develop a list of steps for dealing with people on the low end of the trust continuum. Indicate that in looking for the cause, they should be as specific as possible. They should describe behavior, not feelings.

If you need additional resources on trust, see the following:

- Donald J. Moine and John H. Herd, *Modern Persuasion Strategies: The Hidden Advantage in Selling.* Englewood Cliffs, NJ: Prentice Hall, 1984.

- Paul H. Schurr and Julie L. Ozanne, "Influences on Exchange Process: Buyers' Preconceptions of a Seller's Trustworthiness and Bargaining Toughness," *Journal of Consumer Research,* March 1985, Vol. 11.

- Dale E. Zand, "Trust and Managerial Problem Solving," *Administrative Science Quarterly,* 1972, Vol. 17, No. 2.

- David D. Johnson, *Reaching Out.* Englewood Cliffs, NJ: Prentice-Hall, 1992. See Chapter 3.

WORKSHEET: Trust Profile

A Person I Trust		A Person I Do Not Trust
	Name	
	How I Respond to This Person	
	How He or She Responds to Me	
	Impact on Our Negotiations	

WORKSHEET: Action Planning

Directions:

Think about the individual you placed on the low end of your trust continuum. What steps can you take to improve the level of trust between you and this person? Be as specific as you can.

Person

What causes you not to trust this person? Did anything specific happen? What are your feelings about what happened?

Action Steps I Can Take—*What should I do?*

V. Negotiating Styles

Defining the Styles

Objectives:	To introduce participants to five negotiating (or conflict resolution) styles To discuss when and where each of the styles is appropriate
Time:	45 minutes
Group Size:	Small groups of three or four
Materials:	Hard copy of the Negotiating Styles overhead and worksheet for each person. Flip-charts, magic markers, and tape for each group.
Trainer's Notes:	This activity can stand by itself. It is most effective, however, when used in conjunction with a conflict resolution or negotiating styles instrument.
	An excellent review of several conflict instruments can be found in Deanna F. Womack's "A Review of Conflict Instruments in Organizational Settings," *Management Communications Quarterly,* February 1988, Vol. 1, No. 3, pp. 437–445. The article has been reprinted in the *Negotiation Sourcebook* (Asherman & Asherman, 1989), available from HRD Press.

Procedure:

Step I   Display the Negotiator Styles Chart on an overhead projector. Conduct a brief lecture on the five negotiating styles. Lecture notes are provided on page 63. *Allow 10 minutes.*

Step II   After completing the lecture, distribute copies of the Negotiating Styles worksheet.

Step III   Divide the participants into small groups.

Review the exercise: "Discuss each style with the other people in your group. Determine when each style is appropriate to use and when it should be avoided. Ask each group to post their responses on flip-chart paper. Depending on the number of groups, each could take one or more styles to discuss. *Allow 15 to 20 minutes.*

Possible Responses:

Win-Lose—Use at flea markets, yard sales, buying a car, or other times when there will be no on-going relationships with the seller. Do not use when a relationship is important.

Lose-Lose—Use very infrequently, when neither you nor the other party cares about the issue.

Lose-Win—Use when you don't care about the issue and/or when it is important that the other person wins. This may occur when that person has given up a great deal. Do not use with aggressive negotiators, as they will consider you weak.

Win-Win—Use for the majority of negotiations, especially where the relationship is important and it is critical to find a solution that meets the needs of both parties.

Compromise—When time is at a peremium or when goals are only moderately important and not worth the extra effort.

Step IV   *Reporting Back*
Ask each group to report on one of the styles.

LECTURE NOTES: Negotiating Styles

In delivering your lecture, make the following points. Give as many examples as you can. Current events or company issues are ideal examples.

- There are five basic approaches to negotiating with others and dealing with conflict.

- In dealing with conflict, we are usually concerned with three conflicting needs: (1) to be assertive to ensure that our own needs are met, (2) to be responsive to the needs of others, and (3) to maintain the relationship.

- At this point, give an example from your own experience. Select something to which everyone can relate.

- Display the Negotiations Styles Chart on the overhead (see next page). Distribute copies of it to the group, if you have not already done so.

- The five basic negotiation styles:

1. **Win-Lose (Competitive).** A person with this style is very competitive; he or she is basically saying, "I want it all. I really do not care about you. You are not important nor is our relationship."

2. **Lose-Win (Accommodating).** This negotiator is saying the relationship is critical: "I am willing to put aside my own needs and interests to make you happy." The lose-win style is the exact opposite of the competitive style.

3. **Lose-Lose (Avoiding).** This style is somewhat similar to the lose-win style. This person is not participating. His or her approach is "whatever": "Whatever you want is fine by me." The negotiator is very passive and is not concerned with the content or the relationship.

4. **Win-Win (Collaborative).** This person has figured out how to be both assertive and responsive. He or she is a very tough, but principled, negotiator—one who is tough on the issues but relatively easy on the other party.

5. **Compromise.** This person has a lot of very good skills but is probably not as assertive or creative as the collaborative negotiator. He or she moves too quickly to "split the difference."

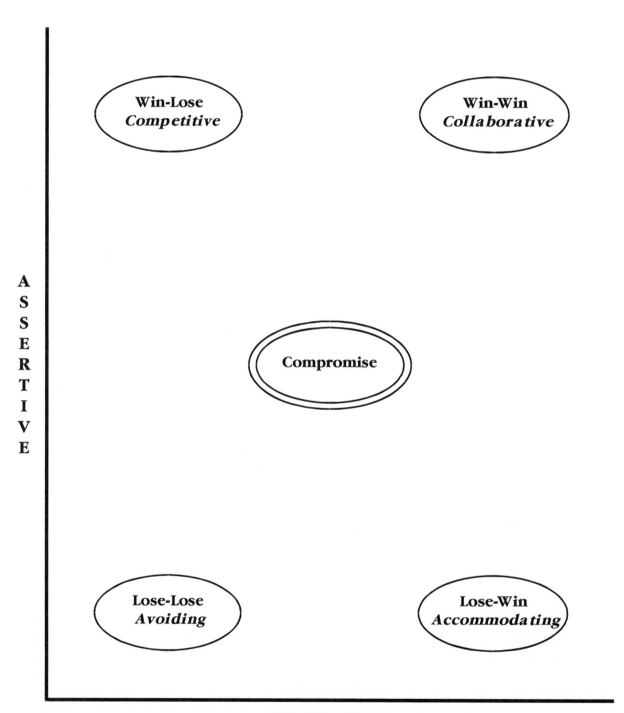

NEGOTIATING STYLES

Negotiation at Work: Maximize Your Team's Skills with 60 High-Impact Activities, ©2012 HRD Press.
Published by AMACOM Books, American Management Association, www.amanet.org.

WORKSHEET: Negotiating Styles

Style	When to Use	When Not to Use
Avoiding		
Accommodating		
Competitive		
Collaborative		
Compromise		

Negotiation Styles Practice—Long Version

Objectives:	To highlight different negotiation styles To understand the impact of the *competitive*, the *accommodating*, the *avoiding*, and the *collaborating* styles on negotiation outcomes
Time:	70–90 minutes (per style)
Group Size:	16–20 people divided into groups of three.
Trainer's Notes:	The same procedure should be used for all four styles. One option is to have both role-players play the same style. Utilize any role-play that you have available. Two role-plays may be found in the Appendix.
Procedure:	
Step I	Explain to the group: "The purpose of this exercise is to experience the various styles and how to cope with them. We will begin with the competitive style. "We will divide into groups of three. In each group, one member will observe as the other two engage in a role-play. One player should use his or her personal negotiating style during the role-play, while the other should adopt the competitive style. Hand out the Observer Sheet to the observers. "We will repeat this process with each of the following styles: *accommodating, avoiding,* and *collaborative.* "Those of you who play the negotiators according to a given style will receive a set of suggestions on how to play the role. You can feel free to utilize additional behaviors." Check for questions. *Allow 5 minutes.*
Step II	Distribute copies of the Style Notes to the members who role-play the competitive negotiators. While the negotiators are preparing, brief the observers. Cover the following: *Allow 10 minutes for preparation.* • "Your job is to observe, not to intervene." • "Notice how the competitive behavior shows itself." • "What impact does the behavior have on the negotiation?"

- "What behavior does the other party use? Is he or she able to diffuse the competitive behavior? If so, how?"

- "Your assignment will be to lead the group discussion at the conclusion of the role-play."

Step III Begin the role-play. The objective is not to complete the exercise, but to highlight the behavior and how it is dealt with. Allow 10 to 15 minutes.

Step IV Stop the action, then ask the observer to lead the debriefing. Make sure to ask the role players to share their reactions. Remind them to give special attention to what went well and the impact of the assigned styles on the process. Allow 10 minutes.

Step V *Reporting Back*
- Have each group report on what the competitive negotiator did. How did she or he demonstrate the behavior?

- How did the other party deal with the behavior?

- What went poorly? What went well?

- What was the impact of the negotiation on their effectively solving the problem? *Allow 20 to 30 minutes.*

Note: You should post these questions for the group's reference.

Step VI *Building a Model*
After the small groups have given their reports, ask the group to build a list of ways of dealing with a competitive negotiator, based on what went well during the role-play negotiations. They should also identify what behaviors to avoid. *Allow 15 minutes.*

Note: Remember: repeat this procedure with each negotiating style.

Observer Sheet

Directions:

Your job is to observe, not to intervene. At the conclusion, your assignment will be to lead the group discussion and observe the following:

- How did the competitive behavior show itself?

- What impact did the behavior have on the negotiation?

- Is the other party able to diffuse the competitive behavior? If so, how? Give specific examples.

- What was done well that was helpful?

STYLE NOTES: Competitive Style

The following behaviors are only suggestions. You may add others if you wish. Behaviors you should use:

- Insist that your approach is the correct one.

- Interrupt the other party.

- Focus on the person, not the issues. (For example, say "I think *you are* wrong about. . . .")

- Don't give any reasons for your actions or statements.

- Use put-downs and insults.

STYLE NOTES: Accommodating Style

The following behaviors are only suggestions. You may add others if you wish. Behaviors you should use:

- Apologize.

- Ask what the other party wants.

- Put aside your own needs.

- Respond by making statements such as, "Whatever you think will work" and "I'll go along with that."

- Make concessions early—even if the other party does not ask for them.

- Be overly gracious.

STYLE NOTES: Avoiding Style

The following behaviors are only suggestions. You may add others if you wish. Behaviors you should use:

- Act passive throughout the negotiation.

- Just say that you will do whatever the other party wants.

- Repeat that this is not an issue for you.

- Only respond if the other party really pushes you.

- Act as if you do not want to be involved.

STYLE NOTES: Collaborative Style

The following behaviors are only suggestions. You may add others if you wish. Behaviors you should use:

- Ask many questions.

- Listen, and paraphrase.

- Summarize.

- Look for underlying needs and interests.

- Try to solve the problem.

- Ask the other party for ideas and solutions.

- Focus on the problem; make it clear that you see the situation as a joint problem—one that you both will solve.

Negotiating Styles Practice—Short Version

Objectives:	To highlight different negotiating styles
	To identify the strategies for dealing with different styles
Time:	70 minutes
Group Size:	15–20 people, divided into groups of three.
Materials:	Copies of the Style Notes and role-plays for each person.

Trainer's Notes: This exercise is an abbreviated version of Negotiations Styles Exercise 2 and should be used when time is limited.

For this version, assign each group a different negotiating style. For example, if you have six groups, assign two the avoiding style, two the competitive style, and two the accommodating style.

Use the role-play of your choice and the Style Notes from the long version. You could use any of the role plays in this book or from *25 Role Plays to Teach Negotiation,* Asherman & Asherman, HRD Press, 2003.

Procedure:

Step I Explain to the group: "The purpose of this exercise is to experience one of the following four negotiating styles—the competitive, the avoiding, the accommodating, and the collaborative—and to develop strategies for dealing with that type of negotiator.

"We will divide into groups of three and each group will be assigned a role-play situation and a negotiating style. One member should observe as the other two apply their assigned style to the role-play. Although all groups will receive the same role-play situation, the assigned negotiating style will vary.

"You will have 10 minutes to prepare, 10 minutes to negotiate, and 15 minutes to debrief."

Note: One person will be given an assigned style. The other person will play himself or herself.

Step II	Distribute the role-plays, making sure that the styles are evenly divided among the groups.
Step III	While the negotiators are preparing, take the observers outside and brief them on how to observe. Discuss the items listed in the previous exercise. Use the same Observer's Sheet. *Allow 10 minutes.*
Step IV	Begin the negotiation. *Allow 10 minutes.*
Step V	*Debriefing* Ask groups to discuss among themselves how the role-play was affected by the style assumed. What went well? What went poorly? *Allow 15 minutes.*
Step VI	*Reporting Back* Have each group report on how its negotiating style affected the relationship between the negotiators. Ask questions that help participants explore the impact of the different styles on effective problem solving.
Alternative:	One option we have used is to give both role-players in one group the same style. If you do this, do not tell the participants. This can be particularly effective when looking at the competitive and collaborative styles.

VI. Assertiveness

Defining Assertiveness

Objectives:	To define assertive and unassertive behavior
Time:	40 minutes
Group Size:	16 to 20, divided into small groups of four or five.
Materials:	Flip-charts, markers, and tape or pushpins for each group.
Trainer's Notes:	This exercise is ideal for beginning a unit on assertiveness. See the following exercise for the definitions of aggressive and accommodating behavior.
Procedure:	Divide participants into small groups, and ask each group to define each of the following terms:

Step I
- Assertive behavior

- Aggressive behavior

- Accommodating behavior

Ask participants to be as specific as they can and to provide examples of verbal and nonverbal cues to each of these behaviors. Each group should post their examples. *Allow 20 minutes.*

Distribute flip-chart paper to each group.

Step II *Reporting Back*
Ask groups to report back their definitions; then explore the similarities and differences among groups. Try to reach a definition of the three primary behaviors of each style by the activity's conclusion. Place special emphasis on the behaviors that distinguish the assertive individual. Pay particular attention to the distinction between assertive and aggresive. *Allow 20 minutes.*

Note: As an option, have each group select a member who will meet with others in the center of the room to negotiate the three critical behaviors. The objective is to reach a definition of assertive behavior. Be sure to ask each group to choose its most assertive member for this task. Ask the other group members to watch for examples of assertive behavior. You will need additional time if you add this activity.

Practicing Assertiveness

Objectives:	To practice assertive behavior through a written exercise
Time:	40–50 minutes
Group Size:	2 to 3
Materials:	Copies of the worksheet for each person. Flip-chart, markers, tape, or push pins for each group.
Trainer's Notes:	This is a low-threat activity and is a nice follow-up to Assertiveness Exercise 1: *Defining Assertiveness*.
Procedure:	
Step I	If you have conducted *Defining Assertiveness,* indicate to the participants that they will now practice assertive behaviors. If you have not conducted it, then deliver a brief lecture that defines assertiveness and distinguishes among assertive, aggressive, and accommodating behaviors.

Make the following points:

- Assertive behavior is positive: there is a difference between being assertive and being aggressive.

- Being assertive means standing up for your rights without violating or infringing on the rights of others. Being assertive allows you to say no, to give feedback to others, and to demand that you be treated fairly. It is saying, "I, too, have rights."

- Aggressive behavior is often confused with assertive behavior. The essential difference is how you assert your rights. The individual who aggressively responds violates and denies the other person's rights; he or she tramples on others.

- When we are unassertive or accommodating we put aside our own needs—we are afraid to state them for fear of the potential repercussions. Most frequently, we fear that the relationship will be damaged.

Example: If a co-worker came into my office and asked for help that I knew I could not provide, the *accommodating response* would be to say yes and then spend the rest of the day being annoyed with myself. The help most likely would not be given.

The *aggressive response* might be, "I can't believe you! How could you ask something like that? You know how busy we are."

The *assertive response* might be, "I would like to help you, but I just received an additional assignment from management and won't have any time before next week."

Summary
In this example of being assertive, it is all right to say no, but it should be done without putting the other person down.

Step II Distribute copies of the Practice Assertiveness Worksheet. Explain that participants should read the statements in the first column and, for each one, write an assertive response in the second column. Have participants work by themselves. *Allow 10 minutes.*

Step III Divide the full group into smaller groups. Ask members to compare their answers and to select what they feel is the best answer for each statement. They will report this answer to the large group later on. *Allow 15 minutes.*

Step IV *Reporting Back*
Have each group report on its highest ranked assertive behaviors. For each statement, record the behaviors on a flip-chart and hold a discussion. Focus on how well the behaviors met the standard for assertiveness. *Allow 15 minutes.*

WORKSHEET: Practice Assertiveness

Statement	Assertive Response
A co-worker comes into your office and says, "Jack, I need several of your people to work on this project immediately."	
Your boss says, "I don't see any real reason to continue this disucssion."	
Your spouse says, "I can't pick up the tickets you need."	
A hotel clerk says, "We don't have any rooms available in your price range."	
A clerk at a store at which you frequently shops says, "We can offer you a five-percent discount—no more!"	

Being Assertive

Objectives:	To practice making assertive responses
Time:	45 minutes
Group Size:	16–20, divided into small groups of two or three.
Materials:	Copies of the "Being Assertive" worksheet for each person.
Trainer's Notes:	This exercise is a nice follow-up to Assertiveness Exercise 2: *Practicing Assertiveness*. If you do not use it as a follow-up, consult Step I of *Practicing Assertiveness* and deliver the lecture on assertive, aggressive, and accommodating behaviors. This will assure that people have a framework in which to work.

Procedure:

Step I   Distribute copies of the Being Assertive Worksheet. Explain that participants should try to reconstruct dialogue between themselves and another person. They should select a situation they did not handle well—one in which they would have liked to have been more assertive. Give them these directions. "On the left-hand side, reconstruct the dialogue. Write down what they said and how you responded. Then, on the right-hand side, write down how you wish you had responded." *Allow 15 minutes.*

Step II   Ask the participants to share their responses with one or two other people and to provide each other with feedback. *Allow 15 minutes.*

Step III   Close the activity by asking a few group members to share their examples with the class. Encourage the group members to analyze the responses and provide feedback to each other. See if the group can identify the best of the responses. *Allow 15 minutes.*

WORKSHEET: Being Assertive

The Dialogue	What I should have said . . .
They said . . . I said . . .	

VII. Questioning Techniques

Defining Questions

Objectives:	To identify different types of questions
Time:	45 minutes
Group Size:	2 to 3
Materials:	A copy of the Questioning Continuum overhead and Defining Questions for each person.
Trainer's Notes:	If you have conducted previous interviewing programs, use that questioning format.

Procedure:

Step I Deliver a brief lecture on different types of questions. *Allow 10 minutes.*

Use the attached overhead to illustrate your lecture. Make the following points:

- Different questions can have a different impact on the quality of communication between two parties.

- As you move from closed questions to the more open-ended ones, encourage people to share information. Closed questions limit information. Examples of closed and open ended questions are: Closed—"How much do you want?" Open-ended—"Could you tell me a bit more about it?"

- The more information we have, the greater the potential that we can find an answer that works for both parties.

- Give examples of each type of question.

- One should work toward the upper end of the continuum.

Step II Distribute the Defining Questions Worksheet. Explain that they should give an example of each type of question. Ask them to complete the worksheet. *Allow 15 minutes.*

Divide participants in small groups.

If they have other types of questions they want to add, encourage them to do so.

If possible, give each group an overhead transparency of the chart and have them complete one or two questions for reporting back.

Step III *Reporting Back*
Focus on the questions that were developed. Have each group give examples of at least two types of questions. Discuss the likely impact of each queston type on the quality of negotiation. *Allow 20 minutes.*

Question Continuum

Open-Ended Questions

Asking about Feelings or Opinions

Summarizing

Clarifying

Gather Information

Making Judgments

Threatening

Closed Questions

Discourage Discussion

Encourage Discussion

WORKSHEET: Defining Questions

Type of Question	Example
Threatening	
Making Judgments	
Information Gathering	
Clarifying	
Summarizing	
Asking about Feelings	
Other	

Questioning Techniques

Objectives:	To practice asking different types of questions
Time:	40 minutes
Group Size:	3 or 4
Materials:	Questioning Techniques Worksheet for each person.
Trainer's Notes:	This exercise is more effective if used after Questioning Exercise I: Defining Questions. It will not work well if it has not been preceded by an activity that conceptualizes the questioning process. *Allow 5 minutes.*
Procedure:	

Step I   Briefly review the learning points of Defining Questions. Tell participants that they will now practice the questioning process. *Allow 5 minutes.*

Step II   Distribute the Questioning Techniques Worksheet. Explain the directions: "Read through the six statements on your worksheet and record the kind of response indicated after each statement."

Step III   Ask participants to begin work. *Allow 20 minutes.*

Note: Instruct participants to work independently, and then lead a large group discussion. Alternatively, use the small groups and instruct participants to work together. Then conduct a reporting back exercise. Another method, when time is short, is to go through each example with the entire group. Select the method that best fits the time you have available.

Step IV   *Reporting Back*
Ask participants to share their answers, and invite other participants to comment. Ensure that the response is the one asked for. *Allow 15 minutes.*

WORKSHEET: Questioning Techniques

Statement 1

"My people will not go for a deal of this type."

Response—Information gathering.

Statement 2

"Everything you've said sounds agreeable, but I'm not sure that it meets our true concerns."

Response—Clarifying.

Statement 3

"What's important is that we get all of the issues listed and clarified before we begin any real problem solving."

Response—Clarifying.

Statement 4

"Your offer isn't anywhere near what I need."

Response—Information gathering.

Statement 5

"It is not a question of staff, but rather how other people see our group's effectiveness."

Response—Summarizing.

Statement 6

"I don't see how we can complete your project with our current staff, the limited budget, and the very tight time frame you are setting."

Response—Summarizing.

Surfacing Intangibles

Objectives:	To identify the questions needed to surface intangibles
Time:	20 minutes
Group Size:	16–20, divided into groups of 3 to 5.
Materials:	A copy of The Intangibles Worksheet for each person.
Trainer's Notes:	If you have not previously covered the topic of tangibles and intangibles, begin the activity with a brief lecture on this subject. For our purposes, the tangibles are what people say and the intangibles are what people think and feel but usually don't say. Also emphasize that surfacing the intangibles increases the space within which to find solutions.

Procedure:

Step I   Divide participants into small groups of three to five members. Explain that their assignment is to explore what steps a negotiator can take to ensure that the intangibles are brought to the surface during a negotiation.

Step II   Distribute copies of The Intangibles Worksheet. Ask them to use the worksheet to list specific questions that would help a negotiator surface the intangibles. To make the activity more relevant you can tailor the worksheet by editing to include another negotiation, or whatever type of negotiation is the most pertinent to the group or individual. *Allow about 10 minutes.*

Step III   *Reporting Back*
Ask the groups to present the questions they listed. *Allow 10 minutes without the trust discussion, 15 to 20 minutes if you include this discussion.*

Among the possibilities are the following:

- Am I missing something?
- Are you troubled or upset?
- Is there something you're not telling me?
- Is something wrong?
- Do you feel comfortable with the kind of progress we're making?
- There seems to be something you are not comfortable with.
- Can you tell me why you are interested in . . . setting, buying, this deal . . . etc.
- Is there anything else we should talk about?

Initiate a discussion that also includes the topic of trust. Ask participants, "What degree of trust should exist between the two parties?" or "How does trust affect the ability of the parties to deal with intangibles?"

Note: It is common for participants to ask, "What do you do once you know what the intangibles are?" If the group does not raise this question, you should.

Here are some possible responses:

- How you respond is a function of the relationship with the other party.

- Just factor the intangibles into your approach without saying anything.

- Say something to the other party such as "You seem to feel strongly about time. Am I correct?"

Ask participants to share examples from their own experience.

Step IV   Summarize the importance of intangibles: Point out that by identifying them a negotiator expands the negotiating arena, thus creating more possibilities for finding a deal. Also, emphasize that good planning is critical to the success of this process. It is well worth a negotiator's time to think about what the other party may be thinking or feeling. Refer to the planning activities in this book. *Allow 10 minutes.*

WORKSHEET: The Intangibles

Directions:

Make a list of questions and other behaviors that would help surface the intangibles or underlying needs and interests of the other party.

Situation:

You are involved in a negotiation with a very important client. The discussion is not going as well as you would like. You sense there is something bothering the client, but she has not shared what it might be. What steps can you take to get her to talk about what is bothering her? What questions might you ask?

VIII. Ranking Exercises

Negotiator Skills

Objectives:	To identify the skills of the effective negotiator
Time:	35–45 minutes
Group Size:	Small groups of three or four.
Materials:	Negotiations Skills Rating Worksheet for each person.
Trainer's Notes:	This exercise works well with Negotiation Skills 2: *Self-Evaluation*.
Procedure:	

Step I   Distribute copies of the Negotiator Skills Rating Worksheet. Tell the group that, working alone, each participant should rank the items in order of importance. *Allow 5 minutes.*

Step II   When everyone is finished, organize small groups and ask each group to come up with a ranking. They will be asked to report on their three highest ranked items. *Allow 10 minutes.*

Step III   *Reporting Back*
Ask each group to report on their three highest items and to explain their rankings. *Allow 10 to 15 minutes.*

Step IV   Identify similarities and differences between the group rankings. *Allow 5 to 10 minutes.*

Note: There is no correct list of items. However, below are the three issues we believe are most critical and which show up in the literature most frequently:

- Explore underlying needs and interests.

- Plan effectively.

- Be a person whom others trust.

If the issue of knowing when to compromise is raised, stress that many times people move too quickly to compromise and do not obtain the best solution.

WORKSHEET: Negotiator Skills Rating

Directions:

Below are eleven negotiator skills. Rank the skills in order of importance, with 1 being the most important. You will then meet with others to discuss your ranking.

My Rating		Group Rating
——————	Know subject being negotiated.	——————
——————	Plan effectively.	——————
——————	Have high aspirations.	——————
——————	Know when to compromise.	——————
——————	Do not push the other person too hard.	——————
——————	Focus on what the other party is saying—his or her position.	——————
——————	Explore underlying needs and interests.	——————
——————	Clarify your authority.	——————
——————	Know the law.	——————
——————	Be a person whom others trust.	——————
——————	Begin bargaining quickly.	——————

Planning

Objectives:	To identify the characteristics of effective planning
Time:	35–50 minutes
Group Size:	3 or 4
Materials:	Planning Rating Worksheet.
Trainer's Notes:	This exercise works nicely as an introduction to a general discussion on planning, or as the conclusion to a planning module.

Procedure:

Step I Distribute copies of the Planning Rating Worksheet. Tell the group that, working alone, each participant should rank the items in order of importance. *Allow 5 to 10 minutes.*

Step II When everyone is finished, organize small groups and ask each group to come up with a ranking. They will be asked to report on their three highest ranked items. Allow 10 to 15 minutes.

Step III *Reporting Back*
Ask each group to report on their three highest items and to explain their rankings. *Allow 15 minutes.*

Step IV Identify the similarities and differences among the groups. *Allow 5 to 10 minutes.*

Note: There is a great deal in the literature on planning. These are the items that are seen as critical:

- Develop settlement options.

- Think about the other party's situation—put yourself "in his or her shoes."

- Identify underlying needs and interests—both yours and the other party's.

- Clarify your objectives.

Frequently people will suggest working alone. We find that working alone limits the options that are developed. Conversely, working in groups of three gives rise to a greater number of options.

WORKSHEET: Planning Rating

Directions:

Listed below are characteristics of effective planning. Rank the items in order of importance, with 1 as the most important. You will then meet with others to discuss your ranking.

My Rating		Group Rating
_____	Work alone.	_____
_____	Put it in writing.	_____
_____	Clarify your objectives.	_____
_____	Develop settlement options.	_____
_____	Identify what you will accept.	_____
_____	Identify the other party's objectives.	_____
_____	Identify underlying needs and interests.	_____
_____	Work with one or two others.	_____
_____	Think about the other party's situation—put yourself "in his or her shoes."	_____
_____	Clarify your authority.	_____
_____	Develop a list of possible concessions.	_____

Building Trust

Objectives:	To identify the items critical to building trust
Time:	35–50 minutes
Group Size:	Small groups of four or five.
Materials:	A Trust-Building Rating Worksheet for each person.
Procedure:	

Step I — Distribute copies of the Trust-Building Rating Worksheet. Tell the group that, working alone, each participant should rank the items in order of importance. *Allow 5 to 10 minutes.*

Step II — When everyone is finished, organize small groups and ask each to come up with a ranking. They will be asked to report on their three highest ranked items. *Allow 10 to 15 minutes.*

Step III — *Reporting Back*
Ask each group to report on their three highest items and to explain their ranking. *Allow 15 to 20 minutes.*

Step IV — Identify similarities and differences among the groups. *Allow 5 to 10 minutes.*

Note: — We have found three issues to be of particular importance:

- Meet your commitments.

- If you can't meet your commitments, let others know.

- Be consistent.

If you have not previously covered the issue of trust with the group, you might want to close the activity with a brief lecture on trust and its importance. See the resources cited in Skills Exercise 4: *Perceptions and Trust.*

WORKSHEET: Trust-Building Rating

Directions:

Listed below are behaviors that can have an impact on the trust-building process. Rank the items in order of importance, with 1 as the most important. You will then meet with others to discuss your rankings.

My Rating		Group Rating
_____	Be consistent.	_____
_____	Give others credit for their work.	_____
_____	Admit your mistakes.	_____
_____	Admit when you don't know something.	_____
_____	Be fair.	_____
_____	Meet your commitments.	_____
_____	If you can't meet your commitments, let others know.	_____
_____	Be honest.	_____
_____	Be willing to share information.	_____
_____	Don't betray a confidence.	_____

IX. Surveys

Self-Evaluation

Objectives:	To help participants assess their skills in planning and conducting a negotiation
Time:	20–40 minutes
Group Size:	2–3
Materials:	Self-Evaluation Action Planning forms for each person.
Trainer's Notes:	This exercise can be used to open or close the program. The questionnaire can also be distributed prior to the program as pre-work and the survey conducted a second time at the conclusion of the program.
	If you use the questionnaire as pre-work or early in the program, you should hold the Action Planning Worksheets until the end of the program.
Procedure I:	

Step I   *Program Conclusion*
Distribute copies of the Self-Evaluation Survey and Action Planning Worksheet. Review the directions. *Allow 10 minutes.*

Step II   After participants have completed the questionnaire, ask them to discuss their action plans with one other person. *Allow 10 to 15 minutes.*

Procedure II: *Program Beginning*
If you conduct this survey at the beginning of the program, pair people up and ask them to discuss their self-evaluation and to identify one or two behaviors they would like to practice during the program. *Allow 20 minutes.*

SURVEY: Self-Evaluation

Directions

Listed below are the characteristics of the effective negotiator. Review the list carefully and indicate the degree to which you use each skill by circling a number, from 1 for Rarely to 5 for Usually.

Planning	Rarely		Sometimes		Usually

In my planning, do I . . .

	Rarely		Sometimes		Usually
. . . consider a number of potential settlement options?	1	2	3	4	5
. . . look for areas of agreement?	1	2	3	4	5
. . . think about the long-term implications of issues?	1	2	3	4	5
. . . have a target settlement in mind?	1	2	3	4	5
. . . clarify my objectives?	1	2	3	4	5
. . . commit my plans to writing?	1	2	3	4	5
. . . consider the other party's objectives?	1	2	3	4	5
. . . consider the needs and interests of the other party?	1	2	3	4	5
. . . discuss my plan with others?	1	2	3	4	5
. . . know my concessions?	1	2	3	4	5
. . . plan the use of my concessions?	1	2	3	4	5
. . . plan the order in which items should be discussed?	1	2	3	4	5

Face-to-Face	Rarely		Sometimes		Usually

In my planning, do I . . .
When I finally meet the other person . . .

	Rarely		Sometimes		Usually
. . . stay focused on the problem?	1	2	3	4	5
. . . ask questions and listen to the answers?	1	2	3	4	5
. . . clarify the issues before I begin problem solving?	1	2	3	4	5
. . . clarify the other party's proposals before I respond?	1	2	3	4	5
. . . test for mutual understanding?	1	2	3	4	5
. . . periodically summarize?	1	2	3	4	5
. . . explore the other person's needs and interests?	1	2	3	4	5
. . . acknowledge the other person's efforts?	1	2	3	4	5
. . . offer my own proposals?	1	2	3	4	5
. . . solicit proposals from the other party?	1	2	3	4	5
. . . make contingent concessions?	1	2	3	4	5
. . . avoid:					
• being judgmental	1	2	3	4	5
• fixing blame	1	2	3	4	5
• interrupting	1	2	3	4	5
• being patronizing	1	2	3	4	5
• being hostile	1	2	3	4	5
. . . follow my plan?	1	2	3	4	5

Review	Rarely		Sometimes		Usually

After the negotiation, do I . . .

	Rarely		Sometimes		Usually
. . . set aside time to review and assess the results of the negotiation?	1	2	3	4	5

WORKSHEET: Action Planning

Directions:

Using the self-evaluation survey as a framework, list below the changes you will make in how you negotiate.

1.

2.

3.

Trust Assessment

Objectives:	To help participants identify their skills at building and sustaining trust
Time:	20 minutes
Group Size:	3 or 4
Materials:	A copy of the Trust-Building Survey for each person.
Trainer's Notes:	This survey is best utilized as part of a series of activities dealing with trust. It is ideal when used at the conclusion of the other activities. It works nicely in conjunction with Ranking Exercise 3: *Building Trust.*
Procedure:	

Step I   Distribute copies of the Trust-Building Survey. Review the directions. *Allow 5 minutes.*

Step II   After participants have completed the survey, ask them to share it with one other person in the group or retain it for their own information. Another option is to use the survey as a basis for discussion about the factors they see as most critical to building trust. If you select this option with the group, give participants an opportunity to review their survey results. *Allow 15 minutes in small groups.*

SURVEY: Trust Building

Directions:

Listed below are factors critical to building and maintaining a high-trust relationship. Review the list carefully and indicate the degree to which you use each skill by circling a number from 1 for Rarely, to 5 for Usually.

Trust Building	Rarely		Sometimes		Usually
In dealing with others I: . . .					
. . . share information I have about the problems at hand.	1	2	3	4	5
. . . give credit to others for their contributions.	1	2	3	4	5
. . . speak negatively about others when they are not present.	1	2	3	4	5
. . . admit when I do not understand something.	1	2	3	4	5
. . . acknowledge when I make a mistake.	1	2	3	4	5
. . . treat confidential information in an appropriate manner.	1	2	3	4	5
. . . am judgmental of others.	1	2	3	4	5
. . . represent others' positions and ideas honestly and fairly.	1	2	3	4	5
. . . tend to be too critical of others' ideas and proposals.	1	2	3	4	5
. . . always meet my commitments.	1	2	3	4	5
. . . tell people if I can't meet my commitments.	1	2	3	4	5
. . . am always truthful					

X. Case Studies

This section of the book contains mini-case studies, designed to illustrate a variety of issues. Each case should be selected according to your objectives. We frequently use them as an evening assignment in a two-day program.

Each case study is designed to illustrate one or, at most, two learning points. We recommend using three to five case studies at a time.

Follow the steps listed below for each case. *Allow approximately 5 minutes for reading and discussion of each. So if you are using five cases, allow approximately 25 to 30 minutes.*

Step 1. Distribute the case(s).

Step 2. Break into small groups to discuss the case(s). Suggest that they read one and then discuss it, rather that reading them all and then discussing.

Step 3. Conduct a general reporting back and discussion. *Allow 15 to 20 minutes.*

Step 4. Close the session by summarizing the key learning points on the flip-chart.

The directions will provide the learning points for each case.

The Optometry Shop

Objectives:	To look at intangibles and their impact
Debriefing:	When debriefing this case, you want people to realize that the owner is selling his life while the young man is buying a business. They are talking past each other.
Discussion Questions:	• What is the owner selling? • What does the young man think he is buying? • What should the buyer do if he wants to make this sale? • Is there anything he should avoid doing?

CASE STUDY 1: The Optometry Shop

You have been asked to help a friend who is currently involved in the purchase of a business. He relates the following to you:

"I have been trying for some time to buy a small optometry business in my home town. The owner has been in business for some 35 years and has been at the same location for most of that time. The business has been quite successful. I made what I believed to be a reasonable offer. My accountants have thoroughly looked over the business and have talked with his people. I have no doubt that our offer is fair. However, every time we are near a deal, he comes up with another objection or concern. I have reached a point where I'm no longer sure that he even wants to sell the business.

"This has been going on for over three months now, and I'm almost ready to throw in the towel. Either he wants to sell the place or he doesn't—I don't want to, but if necessary, I can look somewhere else. I've told him so."

When you asked him about the seller, he said:

"He's a nice guy. He has built a really good business—one that I think I can use as a solid foundation to build and improve. He's surely done well by it. He put both his kids through college and is clearly respected in the community by just about everyone. His patients all love him. In fact, he has helped many when they were down and out. No one has anything bad to say about him.

"But what good does that do? I still have no idea as to where we are going or even if he will sell the business."

QUESTIONS

- What do you see as the tangible issues here?

- What do you see as the intangibles?

- How do you think the intangibles are affecting the owner?

Purchasing

Objectives:	To look at intangibles and their impact
Trainer's Notes:	This case works particularly well with salespeople.
Debriefing:	When looking at the intangibles, the participants should see the following:

- The assistant director is new.

- She was brought in to "shape this place up."

- She needs to show she is doing something.

- She is probably more comfortable with the vendor she used at her previous firm.

Discussion Questions:	• How might you gather information about this person?

Note: It is important that participants realize they can find out a great deal about someone before meeting him/her.

- How would you handle this negotiation?

CASE STUDY 2: Purchasing

You are about to begin a negotiation with a woman you have never done business with before. She is the new Assistant Director of Purchasing for one of your largest clients. She replaced someone you have done business with for a number of years—an individual who has become a friend as well as a client. Although he is still with the company, he is on a special assignment and will be out of the country for several weeks. Prior to leaving, your friend indicated that this woman had been brought in to help shape up the department.

You have a meeting scheduled for early tomorrow with this woman to discuss a recent proposal you submitted. In a brief telephone conversation, she said, "Your proposal just isn't in the ballpark." This has never happened to you before. Your proposals have usually been accepted as written or with minor modifications at most.

QUESTIONS

- What do you see as the intangibles?

- What impact are the intangibles having on the situation?

Planning Meeting

Objectives: To identify what happens when you feel you have no options

How to deal with a "no-option" situation

Debriefing: When debriefing, ensure that participants identify the critical issue in this case: that the company feels that they have no options (this is mentioned in the next-to-last sentence).

Discussion Questions:

- What is the problem this company is facing?

  Note: Many people will initially see this as nothing more than a money problem. You will have to probe to get them to look beyond this.

- Why won't Felder negotiate?

- Would you negotiate if you were Felder?

- What is the impact of not seeing any options?

- How should they deal with this problem?

  Note: It is useful to point out that many times when people say they have no options, they are really saying that they have strong preferences for a particular person or approach.

  Once the group realizes it is a "no-option" situation, you should ask:

- What steps should the company now take?

CASE STUDY 3: Planning Meeting

You have recently been asked by one of your colleagues to attend a planning meeting about an upcoming company negotiation. Following is the issue as he outlines it.

"We are anxious to have some basic research conducted for us. Everyone has agreed on the need and knows that we cannot get the work done internally. We have neither the people nor the time.

"The research will require three years to do correctly. The best people are in Dr. Felder's department at the state university. After extensive preliminary discussion, we sent them a detailed outline several weeks ago. They subsequently indicated that the cost would be $13 million—approximately three million more than we have budgeted! They also want to re-open negotiations after the second year in case there are 'unanticipated' expenses.

"Since receiving the proposal, we have had two meetings with Felder and the grants people at the university. We explained in detail what our limitations are and asked them to look at bringing the costs down. They have made some very small concessions but none on the overall number. Essentially, their position is, "If you want the work done in three years, that's the price." If we can stretch out the time, they can do something on price. They know that's an unrealistic option—we need this work done as fast as possible.

"I don't see how to get their price into our ballpark. Everyone wants Felder to do the research; he's the acknowledged expert in the field. No one is in his league. We just don't have any options. We also don't have $13 million."

Do you have any suggestions?

Meeting Plan

Objectives:	To learn how to begin a negotiation
	To discuss the steps to take when negotiating for internal support
Trainer's Notes:	There are two critical issues in this case. The first is whether you should begin with the "tough" items first. The second is the need to negotiate with co-workers for support. In the former, we believe you should begin with the easier issues as they help to build a positive climate. As for the latter, when you negotiate for support, give people more time rather than less.
Discussion Questions:	• What do you think of their plan?
	• Would you do anything differently?
	• Where would you begin? With tough issues?
	• What is the advantage of beginning with easier issues?
	• What do you think of their plan for dealing with their co-workers?
	• What do they want from their co-workers?

CASE STUDY 4: The Meeting Plan

Two of your associates approach you and ask for your reactions to their plan for an upcoming negotiation. They relate the following:

"The two of us will be meeting with the folks from General Consulting next week. We had one previous meeting with them, after which they forwarded a letter to us, summarizing the meeting and detailing the items that need to be discussed at the next meeting. Several of the items should be relatively easy, but two may present real problems.

"Our plan is to take on the tough items first. This way, if we don't reach an agreement on them, we don't have to bother with everything else, wasting our time and theirs. We see the tough items as determining the 'scope of work' and deciding who will be assigned to the project. We want a senior person, not one of the new MBAs.

"We want to handle this in a very businesslike way, so we plan to be very clear up front, spelling out exactly what our needs are and what we want. No sense in beating around the bush.

"Our objective is to get the company the best possible deal that is also consistent with the guidelines detailed by the Comptroller's Office. We plan to send the other members of the team a memo summarizing what we've planned and then review it with them at a breakfast meeting prior to the meeting. This will ensure that we are all clear on our objectives and what we want to achieve. Everyone has agreed that the two of us should handle the actual meeting."

What is your reaction to this plan?

The Art Market

Objectives:	To look at concession patterns
Trainer's Notes:	In reviewing this case, pay particular attention to how quickly John made concessions. Point out that there is no evidence that he clarified the buyer's concerns as he went along; he just made concessions.

This case also provides an opportunity to explore the impact of one's emotions on success.

This would be a good time to do a lecture on concessions and concession patterns. |
| Discussion Questions: | • What is John's problem?

• What do you think about how John made concessions?

• Did he clarify the buyer's needs?

• What should he do now? |

CASE STUDY 5: The Art Market

Yesterday, after work, you went to dinner with your colleague John. He was rather depressed and preoccupied by a substantial sale he felt he blew that afternoon. He related the following:

"As you know, the recession has hurt our business and inventory is beginning to get costly; the word from above is to move things at a reasonable price as quickly as possible. So, when an art buyer from a large bank came into the gallery today, I was overjoyed. She wanted to purchase Persian rugs, wall tapestries, paintings, and period furniture for their executive offices, reception halls, and meeting areas. She told me she'd been in every gallery and auction house in the city and not found the quality she had in our gallery.

"After some small talk and a review of her needs, we agreed on three full size Persians, six wall tapestries, two large 10-by-12-foot paintings, a dozen prints, and several period chairs and tables, for which I quoted $425,000. She smiled and offered 50 percent. I launched into my basic appeal about the market value of the items coupled with the tax breaks, compared that figure to the anticipated appreciation of the works in question, and then came down by 10 percent. She noted that the tax appraisal was less than market value on many of the items and that the art market was rather volatile and unpredictable. I responded by calling attention to the historical trends of the art market but still gave her another 6 percent off the basic price. I pointed out that this would leave us with almost no profit and put us in a position of just moving goods at cost."

You asked John what happened next.

"She indicated that she really liked the goods but that her budget was just too limited. I asked her what else she needed, and she mentioned a number of items we don't carry. In an effort to close the sale, I offered to absorb the delivery charges and to have our people help in the hanging. She seemed to be wavering, and so, to sweeten the deal, I offered to frame the tapestries, since she was concerned with what would happen to them in a public area.

"Then, all of a sudden, she began to look very unsure and indicated she would have to review this with her client and would get back to me.

"I can't figure out what happened. I know she had the authority to purchase."

When you asked what he did then, he said:

"What else could I do? She said she would be back. Now I just hope she calls. What happened? Should I have done anything different? I just don't know."

What advice do you have for your friend?

The Condominium

Objectives: To explore how to respond to a "problem" in a negotiation

Trainer's Notes: In reviewing this case, there will be some participants who feel that "if the friend wants the condo—if it's in his price range—he should take it. In a situation like this, you don't want to begin looking again."

Others will argue that the seller's response is only a tactic and that he should test it. If it is refused, he can always take the current deal.

Discussion Questions:
- How was it handled?

- Should he call back?

- If he does call back, what should he say?

- Should he ask to talk with the client?

- Why not take the deal?

CASE STUDY 6: The Condominium

You are at a friend's home when the phone rings and he engages in a discussion over a condo he is thinking of buying. After he gets off the phone, he asks your opinion about how he handled it and what should be done next.

He relates the following:

> "I looked at this condo last week. The agent asked $275,000. My initial offer was $245,000. Then, after some discussion and several offers, I made an offer of $250,000. The agent indicated he thought he could sell that to his client and would get back to me. When he called he said that his client would not go for the price and that we had a problem. He asked what I thought we could do. I told him I would think about it and get back to him."

When you asked how badly he wanted the place, he said that it was one of the nicer ones but that he really didn't want to go over $250,000, even though he could afford to do so. He also indicated that he didn't want to start looking again.

What should he do?

The Antique Car

Objectives: To explore negotiation openings

To respond to an unsolicited opening

Trainer's Notes: There frequently is mixed opinion on this case. Some members of the group will want to take the money. They will point out that the seller doesn't need a higher amount and doesn't know what else is available.

Others will argue this is just an opening and that the buyer will clearly go higher. They argue that the seller should disregard the buyer saying that he doesn't like to haggle; they believe it is a ploy.

Others will suggest that the buyer is clearly interested. They feel the seller should invite him to talk and that after the buyer is given more information about the car's features and condition, the seller can probably move the price up. The buyer should be encouraged to talk.

Discussion Questions:

- Should the seller take the offer?

- What are the implications of the seller not taking the offer?

- Is this just an opening?

CASE STUDY 7: The Antique Car

As the result of a series of financial reverses, you are faced with selling a portion of your antique car collection. You need to get at least $65,000, and you need it in three days.

The car you have up for sale is an antique Bentley that is in excellent shape and you know is easily worth $85,000, if not more. You haven't checked on the market value or whether there are any people looking nor have you placed any advertisements. While you are discussing the situation with your spouse, a well-known collector approaches. After some brief conversation, he indicates that he has heard, through mutual friends, of your interest in selling the Bentley. As the two of you are looking at the car, he says, "Look, I don't like to haggle—it's not my style. I can give you $74,000 for the car, and I can have a bank check to you in 24 hours."

What do you do?

The New Car

Objectives:	To illustrate developing needs and interests and how to address them
Trainer's Notes:	Many participants will bring to this case their own experience in buying a car and will feel that no room is available for negotiation. Urge the group members to talk about their experiences. People are always buying cars and find this enjoyable.
Debriefing:	Ask these questions during the debriefing:

- What information do you need to find out?

- What questions should you ask?

- How would you develop the climate?

- What currencies do you have? How would you develop them?

- What currencies does the owner have available?

CASE STUDY 8: The New Car

You just found the ideal new car: a dark green Jeep Grand Cherokee Limited sitting on the lot at Classic Motors. It's exactly what you want. You travel quite a lot in the New England area and the four-wheel drive, as well as the luxury, appeals to you.

The dealer is close to your home and has an excellent reputation for honesty and good service. The dealership provides free loaner cars if you need service. Your old car is going to your nephew, since he is just getting his license. Your bank has already approved your credit and you have the necessary down payment. The problem is that this dealership is asking $800 more for the car than a dealership across town. You would like to buy from Classic but want to get the best deal possible.

You will be sitting down with the Classic owner/manager in about 20 minutes. He is in the same golf league as you, and your daughters are friends. After a discussion with your spouse, you both agreed that you would buy from Classic if they would take at least $400 off their current price.

QUESTIONS

- What do you need to find out from the owner/manager?

- What questions would you ask to get that information?

- How would you develop the climate? Be specific.

- Is there any additional information that you should obtain?

The Client Meeting

Objectives: To explore the need to be specific with those whom you represent

To explore the impact of not asking for specifics

Trainer's Notes: Many participants will feel "the client trusts you, so don't worry; everything will work out." It is important that people realize that the failure to be specific can later lead to confusion and misunderstanding.

As part of the discussion, help participants understand that this can also happen when they represent their company or department in negotiations.

Discussion Questions:
- What are the implications of going forward based on what has been said?
- Is there a downside to proceeding?
- Under what conditions should you proceed?

CASE STUDY 9: The Client Meeting

You are meeting with a client to talk about an upcoming negotiation that you are conducting for him. You have discussed the objectives, needs, and interests of both your client and the other party. You have even discussed your fee, which is substantial. In fact, it is the most you have ever received for representing someone.

In an effort to bring the meeting to a close, you ask the client to be specific in detailing what he needs from this negotiation.

He responds with the following: "Listen, I trust you. We have talked at length, and I am sure you have a good sense of what I need and what the business requires." When you begin to protest, he cuts you off by saying, "Look, don't worry. I am sure we will be happy with what you bring back for our approval."

How should you respond?

The Bid

Objectives:	To determine how to respond to a negotiation opening
Trainer's Notes:	This case is ideal when used with salespeople. It is important to help people see that this is not the time to drop your price, but the time to utilize your interviewing skills to probe for information.
Discussion Questions:	• Why not do what he wants?
	• What are the implications of saying yes?
	• What other options are available?
	• Can you afford not to say yes?
	• What other possibilities are available?

CASE STUDY 10: The Bid

Your company is one of four that have been asked to bid on a large multimillion dollar supply contract for a major defense contractor. You submitted a proposal that you felt was honest and fair.

The company then asked that everyone re-bid, this time using a new specification worksheet they developed so that they could more clearly compare the bids. You completed the worksheet and sent it back.

A few days later, you received a call from the firm indicating that you were in the lead. They said they would like to give you the job, but that you would have to reduce your price by at least 10 percent.

How do you respond?

Increasing Overhead

Objectives: To discuss what to do when the other side quotes someone who is not in the room

Trainer's Notes: In this kind of situation, a negotiator should delay the start of the negotiating process, find out who paid 42 percent, and contact them for details. Some participants will probably object to this response, stating that the other party will get the impression you are calling him or her a liar. Discuss how to pursue this course of action without giving the other party such an impression.

Discussion Questions:

- Should you pay the 42 percent?

- What are the implications of saying yes?

- Do you have any options?

- What if you decide not to pay?

- What do you do when someone quotes someone who is not in the room?

CASE STUDY 11: Increasing Overhead

Recently, overhead charges at all research sites have been increasing dramatically. In some instances, they have added almost 50 percent to the overall cost of the new product research your company does. This problem has become particularly acute at the larger, most prestigious institutions where you usually fund several different projects.

Last week, you met with a representative from one of these institutions. During the meeting, you told him that your firm would only pay 20 percent for overhead. You were somewhat taken aback when he told you that one of your associates from another department had agreed to an overhead of 42 percent just the previous week, and he expected you would pay the same.

How should you respond?

Telephone Components

Objectives:	To look at the issue of risk taking
Trainer's Notes:	This case is also ideal for salespeople. Groups are frequently divided on this case. Many feel you should probe the issue and see if you can meet with some of the vice president's people while he is away. Others argue that you have been waiting too long for this company and that you should give him a price and get in the door.
Discussion Questions:	• Can you afford not to give the vice president a price?
	• Is there a downside to giving him a price?
	• What options are available?

CASE STUDY 12: Telephone Components

You are a manufacturer of high-technology telephone components. Your firm is relatively new, but you have obtained contracts to supply a number of the industry's smaller manufacturers. You have yet to establish business with any of the "major firms," but if you are to grow, or even survive, that has to happen, and happen soon.

Yesterday, you received a call from the secretary to the Senior Vice President of Manufacturing of one of the industry's largest firms. You have had two previous appointments with the person, both of which he canceled at the last minute. The secretary indicates that the vice president can meet you at the University Club for about one hour before he leaves on an important overseas trip.

You arrive on time and there is a message waiting for you: the vice president's prior meeting has been extended, but please wait and he will be there. About 20 minutes later he arrives, indicating that he is really pressed for time. After some small talk about each other and your firm, he says, "Look, I'm leaving on a three-week business trip, and I have to get going, but we would like to give your firm a try. What's your best price on a six-month contract to produce tone mechanisms?"

How do you respond?

XI. Negotiation Transcripts

The A/V Shop

Objectives:	To illustrate:

- Openings and how to make them

- Concession and its use

- Closings

Time:	50–70 minutes
Group Size:	Small groups of 3 or 4
Materials:	A copy of the script for each person.
Trainer's Notes:	This is a long transcript and works well as an overnight activity. If you have given this as an evening activity, move right into Step II, the small group discussion. Another possibility with this exercise is to ask two participants to read it aloud while others use the handouts to follow along. This approach is effective when the transcript has not been given as an overnight activity.
Procedure:	
Step I	Distribute copies of *The A/V Shop*. Instruct participants to read it independently and to answer the questions at each stop point. *Allow 15 to 20 minutes.*
Step II	After they finish, divide them into small groups for group discussion. *Allow 20 to 30 minutes.*
Step III	*Reporting Back—Allow 15 to 20 minutes.* Deal with each stop point separately. The key points for each are as follows:
Question 1:	*If you were Charlie, how would you respond to Bill Miller?* Questions to ask:

- What is Miller really asking?

- Do you give him a price at this point?

- Why or why not?

Answer:	Miller is basically asking for a price which you should not give until you know exactly what he wants to buy.

- What question should you ask Miller?

Answer:	What are you looking to buy?
Question 2:	*How effective was Charlie's opening?*

Questions to ask:

- What was wrong with Charlie's opening?

- What would have been more effective?

Answer:	Charlie's opening is too tentative. By prefacing your price quote with, "I was thinking of" you are clearly saying the price is negotiable. The best approach is to list all the items for sale and then your price. This eliminates any possible confusion and defines what the price covers.
Question 3:	*How effective was Bill Miller's use of concessions? Is he in a good negotiating position?*

Questions to ask:

- Has Bill Miller used his concessions well?

- Has he received anything for his concessions?

- What do you think about his pattern of concessions?

- Is the pattern effective?

Answer:	Basically Bill has made his concessions too quickly. They suggest that he is anxious. Also, he has not received anything for his concessions. Concessions should be thought of as currencies: you don't give them away for nothing, you want to get something in return.
Question 4:	*How do you think Charlie has handled Bill Miller's effort at reaching a settlement?*
Answer:	Very well. He confirms what he really wants and that he has made concessions.

Question 5: *What happened that allowed them to reach a settlement?*

Questions to ask:

- What did Bill Miller do?

- Why did Charlie say yes?

Answer: Basically Miller found a way to expand the pie. He provided Charlie with psychological income. He gave him value.

Note: We have only highlighted a small number of the issues raised in this case. You should feel free to expand the discussion. When covering Section 4, you might discuss the pressure the buyer is putting on Charlie. Also, look at whether either of them really have options. Although they both imply they do, they probably don't, since they are not moving to exercise any options.

Step IV Conclusion

Summarize the key learnings or ask.:

- If you were Charley, what would you do differently the next time?

- If you were the buyer, what would you do differently the next time?

TRANSCRIPT: The A/V SHOP

Notes	Script
	Seller: So, Mr. Miller, what do you think? It's a pretty nice shop. That camera equipment, that's "A"–number–one tops and the . . . other stuff . . . the recording stuff . . . that is just state of the art.
	Buyer: Yeah, yeah, it's OK. It might be what I'm looking for. I don't know, Mr. Stone.
	S: Charlie. Charlie's the name. Now you relax, and let's talk.
	B: I'm Bill Miller. It's good to meet you. So, I hear that you're going out of business.
	S: No, I'm not going out of business. I'm just going to make a change, that's all.
	B: Good for you. What are you going into?
	S: I'm going to open up an antique shop.
	B: Wow! You're into antiques?
	S: I'm very serious about collecting. In fact I go to all the auctions . . . and it's, well, it's about time in my life that I do something that I really like.
	B: Sounds great. Say, Charlie, are those video cameras the most recent models?
	S: Oh, sure. In fact, that's the new line that CBJ turned out last year.
	B: Yeah, I know. I'm familiar with their line.
	S: Well, then you know that it's very good equipment.
	B: Yeah, yeah, it's very well rated. So, Charlie, what are you looking for?

Question 1: If you were Charlie, how would you respond to Bill Miller?

	S: You mean price?
	B: Yeah.

Notes	Script
	S: Well, you know, before I can give you a realistic price, I'd like to know what it is that you're looking for.
	B: Well, Charlie, I'll tell you. I've got some capital I'd like to invest, and I think that a retail business would be a good idea. I know the A/V business, as a producer. I also have some background in video. So, I'd like to buy you out. The whole business.
	S: OK, Bill. Just one thing. I've promised my brother-in-law the rental part of the business. I don't mean the equipment. I mean just the, you know, the goodwill trade with the hotels and the other people that rent.
	B: That's fine with me. I'm just interested in the equipment. You know, cameras, screens, projectors, overheads. So, what's your asking price?
	S: I was thinking of $65,000.

Question 2: How effective was Charlie's opening?

	B: Isn't that a little high?
	S: No. The equipment is new. It's all in great shape. It's the best quality, and I think you'll find the price competitive.
	B: Now Charlie, I've already checked around, and I know your equipment has been on the market for several months now, and that it's comparable to stuff out there that's going for a lot less.
	S: Oh, but not the same quality.
	B: It is.
	S: It is not . . . uh . . . sorry . . . uh, what are you ready to offer? You know, you make me an offer.
	B: Well, I don't want to go over 50 thousand. Now look, I've already looked at some equipment that was pretty similar to yours, and it was right around 50, so that's the ballpark I want to stay in.
	S: Bill, I've. . . I've already been offered more than 50 thousand. I'd be very surprised if the cameras you saw were as new or of as high quality.

Notes		Script
	B:	Now Charlie, you've been trying to sell for two months now, and you haven't been able to move it. Now look, you want to go into something new, I'm prepared to take the shop off your hands right away if we can agree on a price.
	S:	Wait a minute. I'm not in that much of a hurry. I've decided for change, it's very true, but 50 thousand . . . that's certainly not in my ballpark. I can wait for a little while longer and see how much more I can get.
	B:	OK, Charlie. What would be in your ballpark?
	S:	As I said, $65,000 would be in my ballpark.
	B:	Charlie, I think it's high. I mean, you've been trying to sell for two months. While you sit on this deal, you're losing money. Look, if we can make a deal today, I'll pay you 52 thousand.
	S:	Now Bill, that's just not enough. You know, I … I can throw in some support services to get you started until you become familiar with the business.
	B:	Now look . . . I don't think I'll need any support. I'm pretty familiar with the business.
	S:	Well . . . how would you go about paying for this? I mean, how much cash?
	B:	Well, I was thinking, a down payment when we make the deal and the balance in 30 days.
	S:	Oh, no, no, no. You know, if you were talking cash . . .
	B:	OK. Look, I can pay you cash. I'll tell you what I'll do. I'll pay you 50 percent cash and the balance in 30 days.
	S:	Thirty days! Bill, that's another month!
	B:	OK, Charlie. Fifty percent on contract and 50 percent in five days if you can deliver in five days. Charlie, what can you do for me with those terms?

Question 3: How effective was Bill Miller's use of concessions? Is he in a good negotiating position?

	S:	In that case, maybe I can go to 61 thousand, but that's with the understanding that you pay 50 percent in cash, up front.

Notes		Script
	B:	Charlie, Charlie . . . look: I'm still trying to get this closer to 52 thousand.
	S:	Not for this quality. Remember, that equipment today would go for upwards of $90,000. And you'd have to wait forever for delivery. My stuff is available right now.
	B:	Charlie, so is the other stuff I've looked at. Now come on . . . I'm paying you 50 percent cash up front. You can do better than 61 thousand.
	S:	Well, I might be able to go to 59 five, but that's the best I can do.
	B:	Charlie, I can take this stuff off your hands right away. I can get cash to you in 24 hours, so you can go into your other business. You're not gonna have another thing to worry about once we've completed this deal. Now Charlie . . . that's a lot of peace of mind I'm offering you.
	S:	I don't know. Uh, let . . . let me sit on it for a day or two. I . . . I have some other people coming in . . . and let me see what I can do with them . . . and I'll let you know in a day or two.
	B:	Aw, I don't know. I mean, you're talking about another few days to make up your mind. That few days becomes a week, and before you know it you've sat on the equipment another what . . . 45 to 60 days.
	S:	Uh, no, no, no, no . . . that's not true. I'll . . . I'll decide soon. It's just that I've had a couple of other offers. I want to make sure that I'm getting the best money for my equipment that I can.
	B:	You know, we're so close. Look, why don't we just strike a deal now. We're not talking about that much of difference.
	S:	No, we're not, but you'll have to improve that 52 thousand. I mean, I've got some other people coming in, as I told you, and I've been . . . I'm not that pressed, and I've been offered better than 52 thousand.
	B:	You're not pressed? Yeah. You could put this stuff down in your basement and not even bother to sell it.
	S:	You still need to come up more toward that 59 . . . meet that 59 thousand, five hundred. Remember, Bill, I've already taken $5,500 off my original asking price.
	B:	Charlie, I can pay you 50 percent cash and I can get it to you in 24 hours.

       Negotiation at Work: Maximize Your Team's Skills with 60 High-Impact Activities, ©2012 HRD Press.
Published by AMACOM Books, American Management Association, www.amanet.org.

Notes	Script
	S: All you're ready to give me is 52 thousand.
	B: And you want 59 thousand five hundred.
	S: Oh, no, no, no, no, no. I want $65,000. I'm willing to take 59 thousand five hundred, in cash.

Question 4: How do you think Charlie has handled Bill Miller's effort at reaching a settlement?

	B: All right, so where are we? Seventy-five hundred apart? What'll it take to close this deal? Look, I'll tell you what I'll do. I'll . . . if we make the deal today, I'll pay you 54 thousand. How's that?
	S: I'll think about it. In the meantime, I'm going to see if I can get a better offer from these other people.
	B: Charlie, look at what you're giving up—a chance to go into your other business right now. Now look, if we can't come to an agreement today, I can just, you know, go get that other equipment I was looking at.
	S: Are you sure . . .
	B: I'd like to get this thing wrapped up now.
	S: . . . that other equipment is the same quality as mine?
	B: Yes, it is. It's all this year's models. It's in great shape.
	S: The cameras, the recorders, the A/V rental stuff? Everything? All the gear?
	B: Yes, Charlie. You said something about support services before.
	S: You said you didn't need them.
	B: I know, I know, but I just realized something. Now, I've got the inside track on the A/V setup at the auto show that's coming to town. I may need some help with that, setting it up.
	S: Oh . . . that's a biggie! You know, you know I . . . I could help you set that thing up. I know the convention center like the back of my hand.

Notes		Script
	B:	All right, look, I'd have to go outside for help on that. OK. That's great! Look. Look, you supervise the setup for me, and I'll bring my offer up $2,500. Now 56 thousand five hundred, Charlie. How about it?
	S:	All right! You're on! Now let's see. It's $56,500, with 50 percent of that up front, in cash, and you get my cameras, you get the recording equipment, the entire stock. I go ahead and I supervise your setup for you at the convention center. I'll tell you what . . . I'll even throw in the delivery!
		Conclusion

Question 5: What happened that allowed them to reach a settlement?

Ted and Sandy (1)

Objectives:	To identify the behaviors critical to effective issue identification
Time:	35–45 minutes
Group Size:	3 to 4
Materials:	Copy of the script for each person.
Trainer's Notes:	As with the previous transcript, you may choose to have two people read the case. The ideal is to use this transcript in conjunction with Transcript 3: Ted and Sandy (2). Both are brief enough to complete in class. They need not be used as an evening activity. This activity is available on audiotape.
Procedure:	

Step I   Tell the group that they will now analyze a transcript of an interview between two co-workers. Explain that they will work alone first, then in small groups, and that the activity will conclude with a full group discussion.

Step II   Distribute copies of *Ted and Sandy (1)*. Ask participants to analyze it. *Allow 10 minutes.*

Step III   Move participants into small groups. Ask them to analyze and discuss the transcript. *Allow 15 minutes.*

Step IV   *Large-Group Reporting*
Ask the group:

- What happened here?
- Is this typical?
- What went wrong?
- Where do they go from here?
- What should have been done differently?
  Note: Strongly emphasize this question.

The point to make is that the co-workers begin negotiating too soon; they have not clarified the issues. This is very typical of negotiations, and it is likely that many will see this as realistic and feel there is little they can do to prevent it. Many will feel that there is no problem, and ask what Ted and Sandy should do differently. Use this as a way to move to the next transcript exercise. *Allow 20 minutes.*

Step V   Summarize the key learning points; emphasize the importance of clarifying issues before you begin bargaining.

TRANSCRIPT: Ted and Sandy (1)

Notes	Script
	Ted: Hi, Sandy! Good to see you again.
	Sandy: Ted, come on in. How've you been?
	T: Fine, and yourself?
	S: Busy, but other than that, terrific.
	T: Good!
	S: How are things going with you?
	T: As you'd expect, equally busy. I'm sure you've seen our catalog. We've been running a lot of training programs over the last six months.
	S: Yeah, I have seen it, and you've got some really interesting offerings for the coming year.
	T: Well, we've brought on additional people, so now we have the capability of doing a number of things we couldn't do in the past.
	S: Well, it looks good.
	T: Sandy, in your memo you indicated that you had some interest in putting together some PC training.
	S: Yeah, a while back we bought PCs for everyone in the department. Now I find out that they're just not being used. So what I want to do is put together some kind of training program that'll teach people how to use them.
	T: Mmm . . . that's something we've never done before, but one of the new people we brought on is a woman who did PC training at her old company. In fact, one of the reasons we brought her on was the anticipation that this type of training would be needed here. We've now got the capability to do a good job for you.
	S: Good, Ted. Let me tell you a little bit of my thinking on this. Jack over in Data Processing and I have done some talking, and I'd like to bring in some of his people to help.

Notes	Script
	T: Well, I'm not quite clear on why you'd want Jack's people. I mean, they're involved in doing data processing, but they've never done any training—none at all.
	S: Agreed, but I thought that your department would have the experience and knowledge in the training area, and that I could bring in their people for their knowledge of computers—you know, the technical part of the session.
	T: It really won't work that way.
	S: Why not?
	T: Well, when we do training sessions, our people learn all they need to before they run them, and as I told you, we have somebody new who knows computers.
	S: But I've already discussed this with Jack . . .
	T: Sandy, that's not the issue.
	S: What is it, then?

Questions:

- How was this handled?

- What went well?

- What was done poorly?

- Could anything have been done differently?

Ted and Sandy (2)

Objectives:	To identify the behaviors critical to effective issue identification
Time:	35–45 minutes
Group Size:	3–4
Materials:	Copy of the script for each person.
Trainer's Notes:	For maximum impact this transcript should follow *Ted and Sandy (1)*. However, it can be used alone. This script is available on audiotape.
Procedure:	

Step I   Distribute copies of *Ted and Sandy (2)*. Indicate that participants should first read the transcript on their own. *Allow 5 minutes.*

Step II   Divide participants into small groups and ask them to analyze Ted and Sandy's situation. *Allow 10 minutes.*

Step III   *Reporting Back*
Ask the group what went well. Urge them to be as specific as possible. These are among the items they should identify: *Allow 20 to 30 minutes.*

- *Climate Setting.* Ted really seems interested.

- Ted came to Sandy's office.

- Ted is honest in admitting that it's not something they have done before.

- *Issue Identification.* When Sandy begins to get into problem solving, Ted doesn't follow. He says, "Let's go back and figure out what needs to be done."

- He acknowledges her issues.

- She validates his concerns.

- He summarizes the situation.

Note: If you also used *Ted and Sandy (1),* you should compare the differences between the two. Transcript 2 includes these essential differences:

- Ted doesn't argue with Sandy; he acknowledges her efforts.

- He moves to clarify what needs to be done. He asks questions and clarifies his own needs.

- He summarizes the situation at the conclusion of their meeting.

Use the following questions:

- What were the differences between these two situations?

- Which was more effective? Why?

Step IV *Conclusion*
Summarize the activity, make sure to include the following: Good issue identification requires that you:

- Do not begin to bargain right away

- Summarize

- Ask questions

- Clarify both parties' needs

Ask for any final questions.

TRANSCRIPT: Ted and Sandy (2)

Notes	Script
	Ted: Hi, Sandy! Good to see you again.
	Sandy: Ted, come in and sit down. How have you been?
	T: Fine, but very busy.
	S: Yeah, it sure looks like it from your new catalog—lots of new offerings.
	T: Yes, we have some new programs in finance for the non-financial manager, as well as a number of senior and middle management workshops.
	S: Mmm . . . have you added to your staff?
	T: We have. Hard as it may be to believe, we've gotten more staff.
	S: That's really an accomplishment around here.
	T: Sandy, let's talk about your concerns. I was reading over your memo before I came down, and it looks as if you're interested in putting together some PC training.
	S: Yeah, we've got a real problem. Last year we bought everyone their own PC, and for the most part, they're sitting on people's desks and nobody's using them. What I'd like to do now is get a training program in here that would teach people how to fully utilize their computers.
	T: Well, that's not something we've done before, but I think it is something we can be helpful on now. We recently brought in a new person, someone who's been doing this type of work for years at her prior company.
	S: Mmm . . . let me tell you, I've been doing some talking with Jack Stone over in Data Processing, and we've come up with some ideas. I thought that maybe we could involve him or some of his people in putting this program together.
	T: That's interesting, but why don't we wait before we talk about who's going to do the program. Let's go back and figure out what needs to be done in putting the program together. Once we can get this type of list worked out, then we can figure out who should run it.

Notes	Script
	S: That makes sense, let's start.
	T: All right, then. First, I hear you saying that you have some possible interest in having either Jack or some of his people do the training.
	S: Involved in some way, yeah.
	T: All right. From our perspective, one of the things we'd really need to talk about is when you want to get the training done. That's a real critical issue for us.
	S: It is for me too.
	T: Okay, any other issues that you can see?
	S: Well, I guess we better talk about what we're going to teach and the topics we want covered during the program.
	T: That's a good point. I think critical to that is what computers and software packages you're using. From our point of view, I think we need to consider right up front what you see as the length of time you could let people go.
	S: Oh, that's a real concern.
	T: That's always a problem, but I am sure we can work it out. Sandy, anything else you can think of?
	S: No, I think that covers it.
	T: Probably the only other issue that strikes me is how we're going to pay for all this. Whose budget line is it going to come out of?
	S: Should that be number one or number four on our list?
	T: Well, why don't we hold that for a while and come back to it?
	S: Okay, that's probably safest.
	T: Let me see if I can summarize where we are. You're interested in conducting PC training and have some interest in having Jack Stone or some of his people conduct the training.

   Negotiation at Work: Maximize Your Team's Skills with 60 High-Impact Activities, ©2012 HRD Press.
Published by AMACOM Books, American Management Association, www.amanet.org.

Notes	Script
	S: Right.
	T: OK, but we agreed that before we reach any final conclusions on who, we would first look at all the areas we need to cover. That includes both software and hardware, when you want the training completed, how long you think you can devote to the training, and how we're going to pay for it . . . that sounds right.
	S: You take good notes.
	T: Thanks! If that covers everything, we'll look at these issues.
	S: OK.

Questions:
- What went well?

- What was done poorly?

- Should anything have been done differently?

Chris and Kate

Objectives:	To illustrate climate setting and issue identification
Time:	40 minutes
Group Size:	3–4
Materials:	Copy of the script for each person.
Trainer's Notes:	This script is available on videotape.
Procedure:	
Step I	Distribute copies of *Chris and Kate*. Ask participants to review it on their own. Then, divide them into small groups for discussion. *Allow 15 to 20 minutes.*
Step II	*Reporting Back* Discuss the questions at the conclusion of the transcript. *Allow 20 to 30 minutes.*
Note:	For a variation, have two participants read the script aloud. If you use this approach you should still give everyone a copy of the transcript.
Answers: Question 1	*What was helpful from a climate-setting point of view?*

- Chris and Kate spoke about conferences they had attended.

- They mentioned how busy they were.

- They established common ground between them by sharing the above information.

- They referred to the memo, which was also helpful from an issue-identification perspective.

Question 2   *What was helpful from an issue-identification point of view?*

- Chris was ready to answer Kate's questions.

- Kate asked questions

— about time frame

— current procedure

— objectives

— types of reports

— the memo

Kate also

- Clarified

- Summarized

Question 3   *What was missing or left out? Was there anything that should have happened but did not?*

- Kate neglected to let Chris know whether she had any issues to discuss.

- Chris did not ask if she had any issues to discuss.

Step III   Closing
Ask the group to summarize the key learnings.

TRANSCRIPT: Chris and Kate

Notes	Script
	Chris: Hi, Kate!
	Kate: Chris, how have you been? Don't think I've seen you since we attended that conference together.
	C: Yeah, it has been a while, hasn't it? I'm fine, but too busy! How about you?
	K: Fine . . . and also busy. What did you think of that program? Has it been of any value?
	C: Oh sure. Actually, I usually head into those things a bit grudgingly, you know. I resent time away from the job when I'm so backed up with work.
	K: I know, I know . . . me too!
	C: But I have to admit, I always come away with something new and helpful . . . well, almost always.
	K: Yeah, same here. Well, let's see . . . you sent me a memo about setting up a new computer system.
	C: Right, my boss would like to establish a financial planning system. I'll tell you Katie, we are floating in data up to our eyeballs.
	K: More than usual?
	C: Mmm . . . usually, it's only up to our elbows! International has grown enormously, and we just don't have the staff to handle all that additional data. What we need to do is establish a computer-based financial planning system.
	K: What do you want this system to do for you?
	C: Well, we want to be able to look at foreign currency fluctuations and the impact on our cash position. And we need to generate different types of financial reports, and do some financial forecasting.
	K: And how have you been tracking this information up until now? Manually?
	C: Yes.

Notes	Script
	K: And you've been dealing with all these same activities manually? Foreign currency fluctuation, financial reports, and financial forecasting?
	C: Yes, but it's so time-consuming, and the data's increasing. We need to get it all on computer. The time we could save just on reports would be enormous. And, we'd be more up to date.
	K: Sounds reasonable, and it's just the kind of thing we can help you with. What kind of time frame are we talking about?
	C: I need it in three months. That will let us get organized for the next fiscal year. We costed it out and estimated the person-hours required, and my people have already begun to work on the preliminaries.
	K: Well, let me be sure I understand your needs. There's been an increase in the amount of data that International is handling, and you can no longer handle it manually. So now, you'd like to set up a computer-based system to track the data and to generate the same kinds of reports you've been required to do by hand up until now; and this includes tracking foreign currencies and their impact on our cash position while generating financial reports and doing financial forecasting. And, you need the system to be in place within three months.
	C: Yes, exactly.
	K: Fine. There should be the time to do it. Oh, Chris, before we go any further, what kinds of reports do you want to generate?
	C: Well, what we need is pretty standard. Monthly and quarterly sales, share of the market, inventory . . .
	K: OK, that helps.

Negotiation at Work: Maximize Your Team's Skills with 60 High-Impact Activities, ©2012 HRD Press.
Published by AMACOM Books, American Management Association, www.amanet.org.

Question: What was helpful from a climate-setting point of view?

Question: What was helpful from an issue-identification point of view?

Question: What was missing or left out? Was there anything that should have happened but did not?

XII. General Exercises

Negotiation Questionnaire

Objectives:	To facilitate discussion about critical negotiation issues
Time:	30–45 minutes
Group Size:	3 to 4
Materials:	Copy of questionnaire for each person.
Trainer's Notes:	The result of this questionnaire may be covered by a full group discussion or by a small group discussion followed by a large group discussion. We prefer the latter approach.
	Answers to the questions follow the questionnaire. They are for your information; not for general distribution.

Procedure:

Step I Distribute copies of the Negotiation questionnaire and ask participants to complete it. *Allow 5 to 7 minutes.*

Step II *Small group discussion*
Divide participants into small groups to discuss their answers.

Each group should try to reach consensus on the questionnaire items.
Allow 10 to 15 minutes.

Step III *Full group discussion*
Lead a full group discussion. Before discussing each question, determine how many people answered true and how many answered false. Ask people to explain their answers. Before concluding, ask participants if they would like to discuss anything together. Allow 15 to 20 minutes.

Following are sample questions you might ask:

- Why did you answer as you did?

- What troubled you about the other answer?

- Can you explain your answer?

Step IV *Conclusion*
- Ask if there are any final questions

- Summarize any key points that were made

QUESTIONNAIRE: Negotiation

Directions:

Listed below are 12 true-or-false statements. Read through each statement, record your response in the appropriate box, and provide the reason for your response.

1. There is only a minimal correlation between your aspirations for the negotiation and the actual results of the negotiation (what you end up getting**).**

   ❒ True   ❒ False

   Reason:

2. There is an ideal concession pattern.

   ❒ True   ❒ False

   Reason:

3. A negotiation deadlock is a sign that the negotiation has failed or is over.

   ❒ True   ❒ False

   Reason:

4. It is best to begin making offers and counter offers as quickly as possible.

   ❒ True   ❒ False

   Reason:

5.　It is better to discuss the more difficult items last.

❏ True　　　❏ False

Reason:

6.　The time and place of the negotiation are not important if one is clear about one's goals and objectives.

❏ True　　　❏ False

Reason:

7.　Unfortunately, negotiation is made up of winners and losers.

❏ True　　　❏ False

Reason:

8.　Effective negotiators are primarily concerned with addressing their own needs and interests.

❏ True　　　❏ False

Reason:

Negotiation at Work: Maximize Your Team's Skills with 60 High-Impact Activities, ©2012 HRD Press.
Published by AMACOM Books, American Management Association, www.amanet.org.

9.　It is best to get your position on the negotiating table first.

　　❒ True　　❒ False

　　Reason:

10.　Detailed planning should be kept to a minimum, since it tends to limit spontaneity and the ability to respond effectively.

　　❒ True　　❒ False

　　Reason:

11.　Compromise is the best way to ensure that you reach a settlement that meets the needs of both parties.

　　❒ True　　❒ False

　　Reason:

12.　Trust is essential if the two parties are to negotiate effectively.

　　❒ True　　❒ False

　　Reason:

Questionnaire Answers

Question 1: *False*

Research strongly suggests that people who come to the negotiation table looking for and expecting more will usually do better. For additional material, see Chester Karrass, *The Negotiating Game.*

Question 2: *True*

The data on concessions suggest that you should not make more than two in a row and that it is best to go from somewhat larger to smaller concessions. A large concession near the conclusion suggests that there is more that could be made.

Question 3: *False*

No! Many times deadlock can lead to a productive change in behavior. It can lead people to rethink their positions and realize that deadlock is not productive for either party.

Question 4: *False*

Research reported by the National Institute for Dispute Resolution and our own observations indicate that when people quickly begin making offers and counteroffers, they limit their ability to understand the needs and interests of the other party. See National Institute for Dispute Resolution Monograph Tactics in Integrative Negotiations by Bazerman, Thompson, Weingart, and Carroll (1988) for additional discussion of this issue.

Question 5: *True*

Beginning with the apparently easier items may allow you to build a sense of trust. In addition, it gets people comfortable with saying yes—making it more difficult to walk away from the negotiation.

Question 6: *False*

One should always be aware of location because it can affect the climate and how comfortable people feel. This does not mean you should always go to a neutral place; there are times you might go to the other person's office if you feel it would make them more comfortable.

Question 7: *False*

That does not need to be the case. We have found that if one of the negotiators surfaces underlying needs and interests, both parties can come out of the negotiation as winners. All too frequently, people argue over positions. Position bargaining leads to winners and losers. See *Getting to Yes* by Fisher and Ury (1981) for a more detailed discussion of this issue.

Question 8: *False*

Negotiators who are interested in seeing that both party's needs are met, that the parties implement their agreement, and that the parties can do business again are usually more successful. Looking out only for yourself tends to lead to position bargaining.

Question 9: *False*

We believe it is best to get the other party to put their position on the table first. When that happens, you learn something about their aspirations and expectations that you didn't know moments ago. However, there are people who feel the exact opposite; they argue that you should always open so that you can take control of the negotiation.

Question 10: *False*

More planning allows you to be more creative because you have given thought to the options—both your own and the other party's.

Question 11: *False*

When people compromise, they frequently give up too much to get the deal. Don't rush to compromise; look for ways to expand the pie so both parties' needs can be met.

Question 12: *True*

If people trust each other, they are more likely to share information. When people do not trust each other, they tend to be more guarded and careful about what they say.

The Melian Dialogue

Objectives: To review the impact of one's power on the negotiating process

Time: 30–45 minutes

Group Size: 3–4

Materials: Copy of dialogue for each person.

Trainer's Notes: This activity can be used as pre-work or between various days of the program. It should not be read during the session. The idea for the exercise came from an article that appeared in the April 1994 issue of *The Negotiation Journal*. The article was written by Heinz Waelchi and Nhavan Shah and is titled "Crisis Negotiations between Unequals: Lessons from a Classic Dialogue." We would strongly urge you to read this article before you use this exercise.

Procedure:

Step I   Distribute a copy of the worksheet, *The Melian Dialogue,* to each participant.

Explain to the group that this dialogue was taken from *The Peloponnesian War,* a work by the Athenian historian Thucydides, who lived in the fifth century B.C. Also explain that for purposes of this exercise, they should assume that the dialogue is historically accurate. After this brief introduction, supply the following background:

"The dialogue represents a negotiation between representatives of Athens and Melos. At the time, Athens was at the height of its power and wanted Melos to become an ally—an offer which the Melians declined to accept, as they did not want to pay tribute to Athens.

"After waiting 10 years for the Melians to change their minds, the Athenians sent a landing force to Melos. The force consisted of 38 ships, 320 archers, and 2,100 heavy infantry. Before they used their force, they invited the Melians to negotiate.

"You are to review the Melian dialogue. What does it tell us about the negotiation process?"

Step II   *Small group discussion—Allow 10 to 15 minutes.*
Post the following discussion questions.

- What does this case tell us about the use of power?

- What else could have been done? Do you see parallels with the use of power today?

- How have the Athenians used their power?

Divide the participants into small groups and ask them to discuss the dialogue. *Allow 15 to 20 minutes.*

Step III   Full group discussion—*Allow 20 to 30 minutes.*

During the discussion make the following points:

- Athens attempts to use its power to force the Melians to accede.

- The Melians, however, feel cornered, since Athens has brought its large landing force to their shore.

- What does this tell us about power and its use?

- What similarities do you see between negotiation in the time of Thucydides and negotiation today?

- What are the implications for us?

Step IV   Have the groups summarize what they have learned.

WORKSHEET: The Melian Dialogue

[85] *Athenians:* Since the negotiations are not to go on before the people, in order that we may not be able to speak straight on without interruption, and deceive the ears of the multitude by seductive arguments which would pass without refutation (for we know that this is the meaning of our being brought before the few), what if you who sit there were to pursue a method more cautious still! Make no set speech yourselves, but take us up at whatever you do not like, and settle that before going any further. And first tell us if this proposition of ours suits you.

[86] The *Melian commissioners* answered: To the fairness of quietly instructing each other as you propose there is nothing to object; but your military preparations are too far advanced to agree with what you say, as we see you are come to be judges in your own cause, and that all we can reasonably expect from this negotiation is war, if we prove to have right on our side and refuse to submit, and in the contrary case, slavery.

[87] *Athenians:* If you have met to reason about presentiments of the future or for anything else than to consult for the safety of your state upon the facts that you see before you, we will stop; otherwise we will go on.

[88] *Melians:* It is natural and excusable for men in our position to turn more ways than one both in thought and utterance. However, the question in this conference is, as you say, the safety of our country; and the discussion, if you please, can proceed in the way which you propose.

[89] *Athenians:* For ourselves, we shall not trouble you with specious pretenses—either of how we have a right to our empire because we overthrew the Mede, or are now attacking you because of wrong that you have done us —and make a long speech which would not be believed, and in return we hope that you, instead of thinking to influence us by saying that you did not join the Lacedæmonians, although their colonists, or that you have done us no wrong, will aim at what is feasible, holding in view the real sentiments of us both; for you know as we do that right, as the world goes, is in question only between equals in power, while the strong do what they can and the weak suffer what they must.

[90] *Melians:* As we think, at any rate, it is expedient—we speak as we are obliged, since you enjoin us to let right alone and talk only of interest—that you should not destroy what is our common protection, the privilege of being allowed in danger to invoke what is fair and right, and even to profit by arguments not strictly valid if they can be made to persuade. And you are as much interested in this as any, as your fall would a signal for the heaviest vengeance and an example for the world to mediate upon.

[91] *Athenians:* The end of our empire, if end it should, does not frighten us: a rival empire like Lacedæmon, even if Lacedæmon was our real antagonist, is not so terrible to the vanquished as subjects who by themselves attack and overpower their rulers. This, however, is a risk that we are content to take. We will not proceed to show you that we are come here in the interest of our empire, and that we shall say what we are now going to say, for the preservation of your country; as we would fain exercise that empire over you without trouble, and see you preserved for the good of us both.

[92] *Melians:* And how, pray, could it turn out as good for us to serve as for you to rule?

[93]   *Athenians:* Because you would have the advantage of submitting before suffering the worst, and we should gain by not destroying you.

[94]   *Melians:* So you would not consent to our being neutral friends instead of enemies, but allies of neither side.

[95]   *Athenians:* No; for your hostility cannot so much hurt us as your friendship will be an argument to our subjects of our weakness, and your enmity of our power.

[96]   *Melians:* Is that your subjects' idea of equity, to put those who have nothing to do with you in the same category with peoples that are most of them your own colonists, and some conquered rebels?

[97]   *Athenians:* As far as right goes they think that one has as much of it as the other, and that if any maintain their independence it is because they are strong, and that if we do not molest them it is because we are afraid; so besides extending our empire we should gain in security by your subjection; the fact that you are islanders and weaker than others rendering it all the more important that you should not succeed in baffling the masters of the sea.

[98]   *Melians:* But do you consider that there is no security in the policy which we indicate? For here again if you debar us from talking about justice and invite us to obey your interest, we also must explain ours, and try to persuade you, if the two happen to coincide. How can you avoid making enemies of all existing neutrals who shall look at our case and conclude from it that one day or another you will attack them? And what is this but to make greater the enemies that you have already, and to force others to become so who would otherwise have never thought of it?

[99]   *Athenians:* Why, the fact is that continentals generally give us but little alarm; the liberty which they enjoy will long prevent their taking precautions against us; it is rather islanders like yourselves, outside our empire, and subjects smarting under the yoke, who should be the most likely to take a rash step and lead themselves and us into obvious danger.

[100]   *Melians:* Well then, if you risk so much to retain your empire, and your subjects to get rid of it, it were surely great baseness and cowardice in us who are still free not to try everything that can be tried before submitting to your yoke.

[101]   *Athenians:* Not if you are well advised, the contest not being an equal one, with honour as the prize and shame as the penalty, but a question of self-preservation and of not resisting those who are far stronger than you are.

[102]   *Melians:* But we know that the fortune of war is sometimes more impartial than the misproportion of numbers might lead one to suppose; to submit is to give ourselves over to despair, while action still preserves for us a hope that we may stand erect.

[103]   *Athenians:* Hope, danger's comforter, may be indulged in by those who have abundant resources, if not without loss at all events without ruin, but its nature is to be extravagant, and those who go so far as to put their all upon the venture see it in its true colours only when

they are ruined: but so long as the discovery would enable them to guard against it, it is never found wanting. Let not this be the case with you, who are weak and hang on a single turn of the scale; nor be like the vulgar, who, abandoning such security as human means may still afford, when visible hopes fail them in extremity, turn to invisible, to prophecies and oracles and other such inventions that delude men with hopes to their destruction.

[104]   *Melians:* You may be sure that we are as well aware as you of the difficulty of contending against your power and fortune, unless the terms are equal. But we trust that the gods may grant us fortune as good as yours, since we are just men fighting against unjust, and that what we want in power will be made up by the alliance of the Lacedæmonians, who are bound, if only for very shame, to come to the aid of their kindred. Our confidence, therefore, after all is not so utterly irrational.

[105]   *Athenians:* When you speak of the favour of the gods, we may as fairly hope for that as your-selves; neither our pretensions nor our conduct being in any way contrary to what men believe of the gods, or practise among themselves. Of the gods we believe, and of men we know, that by a necessary law of their nature they rule wherever they can. And it is not as if we were the first to make this law, or to act upon it when made: we found it existing before us, and shall leave it to exist forever after us; all we do is to make use of it, knowing that you and everybody else, having the same power as we have, would do the same as we do. Thus, as far as the gods are concerned, we have no fear and no reason to fear that we shall be at a disadvantage. But when we come to your notion about the Lacedæmonians, which leads you to believe that shame will make them help you, here we bless your simplicity but do not envy your folly. The Lacedæmonians, when their own interest or their country's laws are in question, are the worthi-est men alive; of their conduct towards others much might be said, but no clearer idea of it could be given than by shortly saying that of all the men we know they are most conspicuous in considering what is agreeable honourable, and what is expedient just. Such a way of think-ing does not promise much for the safety which you now unreasonably count upon.

[106]   *Melians:* But it is for this very reason that we now trust to their respect for expediency to pre-vent them from betraying the Melians, their colonists, and thereby losing the confidence of their friends in Hellas and helping their enemies.

[107]   *Athenians:* Then you do not adopt the view that expediency goes with security, while justice and honour cannot be followed without danger; and danger the Lacedæmonians generally court as little as possible.

[108]   *Melians:* But we believe that they would be more likely to face even danger for our sake, and with more confidence than for others, as our nearness to Peloponnese makes it easier for them to act, and our common blood ensures our fidelity.

[109]   *Athenians:* Yes, but what an intending ally trusts to is not the goodwill of those who ask his aid, but a decided superiority of power for action; and the Lacedæmonians look to this even more than others. At least, such is their distrust of their home resources that it is only with numerous allies that they attack a neighbor; now is it likely that while we are masters of the sea they will cross over to an island?

[110]   *Melians:* But they would have others to send. The Cretan Sea is wide, and it is more difficult for those who command it to intercept others, than for those who wish to elude them to do so safely. And should the Lacedæmonians miscarry in this, they would fall upon your land, and upon those left of your allies whom Brasidas did not reach; and instead of places which are not yours, you will have to fight for your own country and your own confederacy.

[111]   *Athenians:* Some diversion of the kind you speak of you may one day experience, only to learn, as others have done, that the Athenians never once yet withdrew from a siege for fear of any. But we are struck by the fact that, after saying you would consult for the safety of your country, in all this discussion you have mentioned nothing which men might trust in and think to be saved by. Your strongest arguments depend upon hope and the future, and your actual resources are too scanty, as compared with those arrayed against you, for you to come out victorious. You will therefore show great blindness of judgment, unless, after allowing us to retire, you can find some counsel more prudent than this. You will surely not be caught by that idea of disgrace, which in dangers that are disgraceful, and at the same time too plain to be mistaken, proves so fatal to mankind; since in too many cases the very men that have their eyes perfectly open to what they are rushing into, let the thing called disgrace, by the mere influence of a seductive name, lead them on to a point at which they become so enslaved by the phrase as in fact to fall willfully into hopeless disaster, and incur disgrace more disgraceful as the companion of error, than when it comes as the result of misfortune. This, if you are well advised, you will guard against; and you will not think it dishonourable to submit to the greatest city in Hellas, when it makes you the moderate offer of becoming its tributary ally, without ceasing to enjoy the country that belongs to you; nor when you have the choice given you between war and security, will you be so blinded as to choose the worse. And it is certain that those who do not yield to their equals, who keep terms with their superiors, and are moderate towards their inferiors, on the whole succeed best. Think over the matter, therefore, after our withdrawal, and reflect once and again that it is for your country that you are consulting, that you have not more than one, and that upon this one deliberation depends its prospering or ruin.

[112]   The Athenians now withdrew from the conference; and the Melians, left to themselves, came to a decision corresponding with what they had maintained in the discussion, and answered: "Our resolution, Athenians, is the same as it was at first. We will not in a moment deprive of freedom a city that has been inhabited these seven hundred years; but we put our trust in the fortune by which the gods have preserved it until now, and in the help of men, that is, of the Lacedæmonians; and so we will try and save ourselves. Meanwhile we invite you to allow us to be friends to you and foes to neither party and to retire from our country after making such a treaty as shall seem fit to us both."

[113]   Such was the answer of the Melians. The Athenians now departing from the conference said: "Well, you alone, as it seems to us, judging from these resolutions, regard what is future as more certain than what is before your eyes, and what is out of sight, in your eagerness, as already coming to pass; and as you have staked most on, and trusted most in, the Lacedæmonians, your fortune, and your hopes, so will you be most completely deceived."

Framing a Problem

Objectives:	To illustrate the impact of framing on problem solving
Time:	20–30 minutes
Group Size:	15–20
Materials:	Copies of each situation or overheads or slides of each scenario. A copy follows these instructions.
Trainer's Notes:	How a problem is framed can have a significant impact on how the negotiators view the problem, the solutions they reach, and their willingness to take risks. This exercise is based on the the work of A. Tversky and D. Kahneman, "The Framing of Decisions and the Psychology of Choice," *Science,* Vol. 211, 30 January 1981; R. Thaler, Using Mental Accounting in a Theory of Purchasing Behavior, *Marketing Science 4* (1985), 12–13; and Max H. Bazerman and Margaret A. Neale, *Negotiating Rationally,* Free Press, 1992, 32–33. All three publications have similar exercises in them, which you can add to this activity.
Procedure:	

Step I   Divide the group into subgroups A and B. Tell participants that each group will be given a problem to read and then will be asked to make a decision. Tell each group which problem they will be asked to read.

Step II   Distribute the copies of the situations. Make sure that the "A" group receive the A copy and the "B" group the B copy. Have them write down how much they are willing to pay. *Allow 2 minutes to read.*

Step III   Ask the A group how much they would be willing to pay. Post the responses.

Step IV   Ask the B group how much they would be willing to pay. Again post the responses.

Step V   *Note:* What you will find is that the B group participants will always, on average, pay more. Highlight this point.

Step VI   Ask the following:

- What are your reactions to these answers?

- To what do you attribute the differences?

Note: At some point you need to tell them the differences in the scenarios.

When you want to continue the discussion ask:

- What has happened here?

- These problems are pretty similar, why are there differences in what you would pay? Why is this?

- What are the implications for negotiations?

Note: Be prepared to highlight the differences if the class does not.

Step VII   *Lecture*
This brief lecture should be used to summarize the activity. Make the following points.

- Framing is how we describe a problem

- How a problem is framed can affect how people view the potential gains

- We should try to frame situations in terms of the potential gains available if we find an answer

In this case the framing is established by how the places are described.

Step VIII   Ask for any questions.

Summarize. Use an example to illustrate the point.

SCENARIO: The Beach—A

You are sitting on the beach after an afternoon of snorkeling and swimming. It is a wonderful, but hot, afternoon and all you have to drink is a diet soda. As you sit on the beach, all you can think about is a cold beer—your favorite brand. That would make this day perfect.

Your companion needs to call his/her office on the mainland and, knowing how you love your favorite beer, offers to bring you back an ice cold one. He/she tells you that it can only be gotten at the tiny, rickety island shop down the street. Before you can say a word, he/she says to you, "It might be expensive, how much are you willing to pay?"

He/she goes on to say that he/she will only buy the beer if it doesn't cost more than the price you say. If it costs more than that amount, he/she will not buy it. He/she points out that there is no possibility of bargaining with the shop owner.

How much are you willing to pay?

SCENARIO: The Beach—B

You are sitting on the beach after an afternoon of snorkeling and swimming. It is a wonderful, but hot, afternoon and all you have to drink is a diet soda. As you sit on the beach, all you can think about is a cold beer—your favorite brand. That would make this day perfect.

Your companion needs to call his/her office on the mainland and, knowing how you love your favorite beer, offers to bring you back an ice cold one. He/she tells you that it can only be gotten at the tiny, rickety island shop down the street. Before you can say a word, he/she says to you, "It might be expensive, how much are you willing to pay?"

He/she goes on to say that he/she will only buy the beer if it doesn't cost more than the price you say. If it costs more than that amount, he/she will not buy it. He/she points out that there is no possibility of bargaining with the people at the bar.

How much are you willing to pay?

Fairness and Negotiation

Objectives: To define fairness, explore the impact of fairness in negotiation and the impact of an ultimatum on the perception of fairness.

Time: 15–20 minutes

Materials: Ten one-dollar bills

Trainer's Notes: This activity is based on both the works of D. Kahneman, J.H. Knetsch, and R. Thaler, Fairness as a Constraint on Profit, *American Economic Review 76* (1987), 728–41, and W. Guth, R. Schmittberger, and B. Schwarze, An Experimental Analysis of Ultimatum Bargaining, *Journal of Economic Behavior and Organization 3* (1982), 367–88.

Procedure:

Step I Ask two people to volunteer for a brief exercise. Once you have the volunteers, ask them to come to the front of the room.

Step II Give the following directions:

You are faced with the following situation. "I'm going to give person "A" ten dollars to distribute between you. The person may keep any of that amount for him/herself and give the rest to you. Once you have received the proposal, you can choose to either accept or refuse it. If you refuse, both players will get zero. No other conversation is allowed."

Step III *Allow 2 to 3 minutes to complete the transaction.* Remind participants that there is no barganing or discussion—it's one offer.

Note: There are two possible outcomes for this case: (1) Person "A" will offer something approximating 50 percent and Person "B" will accept it or (2) Person "A" will make an offer in which he/she wants most of the ten dollars and "B" will refuse. In the second case, both end with nothing.

Step IV *Discussion—Allow 10 to 15 minutes.*
Note: Your objective for this discussion is to help the group see that not all decisions are economic in nature and that fairness, which each each of us define for ourselves, is also critical.

If "B" refused "A's" offer, ask the following:

Ask "B"
- Why did you refuse?

- By refusing you are getting nothing. Isn't getting something better than nothing at all?

- What type of offer would you have accepted?

Ask "A"
- Why did you make this type of offer?

- What were you trying to accomplish?

- Ask the group for their reactions to what happened.

- Do they agree with "B's" decision to say no?

If "B" accepted "A's" offer, ask the following:

Ask "B"
- Why did you accept?

- What did you like about the offer?

Ask "A"
- Why did you make the offer you did?

- Why didn't you keep it all?

To Summarize
- What are the implications of this exercise for negotiators?

Step V
Deliver a brief lecture that includes the following points:

- People make decisions on factors other than pure economics.

- In considering the offers we make, it is critical to consider the non-economic factors.

- One of the most critical factors is the degree of fairness that people perceive.

- We need to keep this in mind and help people see that you are responding to their needs and concerns and, as a result, the offer is fair.

XIII. Needs and Interests

Needs and Interests Analysis

Objectives:	To identify the differences between (1) positions and (2) needs and interests
Time:	45–60 minutes
Group Size:	Pairs
Materials:	Worksheet for each person.
Trainer's Notes:	Distinguish between positions and needs and interests by using the metaphor of an iceberg. A *position* is a statement that a person makes during a negotiation and represents the portion of the iceberg that is visible. A *need or interest* is often implicit and represents the portion of the iceberg that is below the surface. Needs and interests are often referred to as "intangibles."

Procedure:

Step I   Conduct a brief lecture on positions, needs, and interests. *Allow 10 minutes.*

You can use an example like the neogitations that led to the Camp David accord. During the negotiations, Egypt and Israel each claimed that the Gaza Strip was theirs, thus expressing conflicting positions. The issue for Israel was security; for Egypt it was traditional ownership. The negotiation dealt with the issues, and the resulting compromise allowed for both the security and ownership issues to be resolved (by means of a demilitarized zone).

Use the Defining Needs and Interests overhead to illustrate the concept.

Further define needs and interests as:

- Feelings/beliefs that underline positions

- That which causes a person to feel a certain way about an issue and to express a position on it

Knowing the other party's *needs and interests* can be best accomplished by:

- Increasing trust

- Using open, high-output questions that focus on the *why* behind statements

- Demonstrating a willingness to share your own needs and interests

Step II   Use the following example to further illustrate the differences between positions and needs and interests. *Allow 10 minutes.*

You are negotiating with a prospective new employee about joining your company. The prospect has been with his or her current firm for eight years. Accepting your offer will require the person's spouse and children to relocate. Your company is willing to pay the moving expenses and cover their living expenses until they find housing. The spouse does not yet have a job. The prospect, however, is asking for a great deal more in salary and other payments, as well as a contract, before saying yes. Twice you thought you were near a deal when things fell through.

What do you think might be going on? What could be the underlying needs and interests? Ask the group for their reactions and post their responses.

Other examples drawn from local or national news or a company experience would also be effective to illustrate this exercise.

Once the issues have been identified, ask participants how they would bring the underlying needs and interests to the surface.

Step III Distribute copies of the Needs and Interests Analysis Worksheet. Tell participants that, working alone, they should think about a negotiation they were involved in, either with a client or a co-worker. Ask them to write down (1) the position(s) that they can remember, (2) the needs and interests that they feel were involved but not addressed, and (3) what they think they should have done differently. *Allow 10 minutes.*

Step IV   Pair up the participants and ask them to brief each other on the results of their position/needs and interests identification. Instruct them to put special emphasis on what they might have done differently. *Allow 10 minutes.*

Step V   *Reporting Back*
Conduct a brief reporting back, with special emphasis on those things people might have done differently. *Allow 20 minutes.*

DEFINING NEEDS AND INTERESTS

TANGIBLES

What People Say

Their Position

INTANGIBLES

What People Think or Feel But Do Not Say

Their Needs and Interests

WORKSHEET: Needs and Interests Analysis

Position (What They Said)	Underlying Needs and Interests	How I Should Have Responded

My Needs and Interests

Objectives:	To understand our individual needs and interests
	To understand the impact of our needs and interest on our negotiations
Time:	45–60 minutes
Group Size:	3–4
Materials:	Copies of worksheets for each person.
Trainer's Notes:	This case works well with Needs and Interests Exercise 1: *Needs and Interests Analysis* and Cases 1 and 8. If you have not already presented the lecture on needs and interests (found in Needs and Interests Exercise 1), do so before you proceed with the specifics of this exercise.
Procedure:	Introduce the exercise by telling participants the following:
Step I	"In this exercise we will look at the people who make up our own frames of reference, who affect our behavior.
	"It is important to remember that each person will affect us differently, depending upon the issues being negotiated.
	"Each of us have 'audiences'—people who are watching and waiting to see how we do.
	"Frequently our audiences are not in the room with us, but they still have an impact on our behavior. They influence our behavior. They are our external influencers and will impact how we see see the world. For example, our need to succeed, or to look good in the eyes of others.
	"It is important to understand who our influencers are and the impact they have on us when we negotiate."
Step II	*Note:* if possible, give an example from your own experience.
	Distribute copies of the "Audience" Analysis and "Audiences" and Negotiation Worksheets. Give participants these directions:
	"First, record on your Audience Analysis worksheet the names of the people who make up your audience.

"Then think of a particular negotiation (it does not have to be job-related), and complete the 'Audiences' and Negotiation worksheet, looking at the impact of your Audience on your behavior."

Ask participants to begin. *Allow 15 to 20 minutes.*

Note: Many times when participants work on this exercise they look only at the negatives. Urge people to think also of their positive audience members.

Step III   After the worksheets are completed, ask participants to form small groups and share their experiences with other group members. *Allow 10 to 20 minutes.*

Step IV   *Full group discussion*
Ask participants to discuss the relationship between their needs/interests and their audience, as well as the impact on their negotiations. *Allow 20 minutes.*

WORKSHEET: "Audience" Analysis

Family

Friends

Work

Others

WORKSHEET: "Audiences" and Negotiation

What was the negotiation?

Critical Audience Members	Their Impact

What was the overall impact of my audience on my negotiating success?

XIV. Difficult People

The Difficult Negotiator

Objectives:	To give participants an opportunity to practice dealing with an individual who presents problems during a negotiation
Time:	55–70 minutes for each role-play and the discussion.
Group Size:	3 people
Materials:	Copies of the Personality Profile Worksheet as well as the Role-Play and Observer Sheet
Trainer's Notes:	This activity may be completed with any role-play. You may use one from this book (see Appendix) or from *25 Role Plays to Teach Negotiations,* Asherman and Asherman, HRD Press, 1995. We have used several role-plays and all of them have worked well. This activity is enhanced if you have a particular model for handling problem behavior for the participants to follow. If you do not have a specific model, you should focus your discussion at the end of the activity on those things that worked and those that did not in an effort to build a model.
Procedure:	Note: If you have not already done so, divide participants into groups of three, with one observer and two role-players. The roles will change during the activity so that everyone will have an opportunity to practice negotiating.
Step I	Explain the exercise. Indicate the following:
	"You will have the opportunity to practice negotiating with someone who gives you trouble. In each group, one of you will observe and two will negotiate. Decide who the negotiators will be. One of the negotiators will play him or herself; the other will play a 'difficult negotiator.'
	"I will shortly hand out a personality profile worksheet. The people playing themselves should check the behaviors that the person who gives them difficulty usually demonstrates. Do not check more than five items. You may feel free to substitute items."
Step II	Distribute copies of the Personality Profile Worksheet and the role-play you will be using. Ask participants to complete the worksheet. *Allow 2 to 3 minutes.*
	"When you have finished, hand the worksheet to your partner, who will play that person in the upcoming negotiation."

Step III	Give the following additional directions:

- "The role-play will provide the focus for this activity."

- "For those of you who have been given the personality profiles, incorporate the checked behaviors into how you carry out this role-play. You may feel free to add other behaviors."

- "The observers need to watch the role-play and identify what skills were used in dealing with the 'difficult negotiator.' "

Allow 5 minutes for preparation. While people are preparing, you want to brief the observers. Distribute copies of the attached Observer Sheet.

Step IV	Conduct the role-play. *Allow 10 minutes.*

Step V	Debrief the role-play. *Allow 10 minutes.*

Step VI	*Reporting Back—Allow 20 to 30 minutes.*

Have each group report back. Focus on the negative behaviors and the skills used in dealing with them. Pay particular attention to what worked and what created difficulty. Post this material.

After all the groups have reported back, summarize the key points that were made.

Step VII	Have the groups repeat the process three times, so that each person can practice negotiating with a difficult person. In the second and third tries, have people practice the skills that were previously identified as having worked.

Step VIII	Lead a discussion that summarizes the key points. *Allow 10 to 15 minutes.*

WORKSHEET: Personality Profile

Directions:

Check no more than five behaviors that are typical of someone who presents a problem for you. You will then give this list to your partner, who will use those behaviors in the improvised role-play.

- ❏ Makes demands

- ❏ Doesn't say a word

- ❏ Uses put-downs

- ❏ Questions my feelings

- ❏ Denigrates my concerns

- ❏ Never asks questions

- ❏ Does not listen

- ❏ Threatens

- ❏ Interrupts frequently

- ❏ Is judgmental

- ❏ Focus is primarily on his or her concerns

- ❏ Raises his or her voice

- ❏ Gets up and walks around

- ❏ Makes me defend my position

- ❏ Questions why my position is even an issue

- ❏ _____

- ❏ _____

OBSERVER SHEET: Difficult Negotiator

Directions:

Please answer the following questions about the role-play you observed.

- What went well?

- What behaviors were utilized?

- What went poorly?

- What could have been done differently?

XV. Boundary Roles

The Boundary Role

Objectives:	To determine the demands of the boundry role function
	To explore the impact of the boundary role function on negotiating effectiveness
Time:	30–45 minutes
Group Size:	3–4
Materials:	Boundary Role Worksheet for each person.
Trainer's Notes:	This exercise is particularly appropriate for a homogenous group of boundary role people.

If you are unfamiliar with the literature on boundary roles or with the Adams' Paradox, you should read the following articles:

Cynthia S. Fobian, *Interorganizational Negotiation and Accountability: An Examination of Adams' Paradox.* Iowa: National Institute for Dispute Resolution, 1987.

J.S. Adams, "The Structure and Dynamics of Behavior in Organizational Boundary Roles." In M.E. Dunnette (Ed.), *Handbook of Industrial and Organizational Psychology.* Chicago: Rand McNally, 1976.

These articles can also be used as handout materials for the group.

This exercise can be run by itself; however, it is particularly effective when run in conjunction with Boundary Roles Exercises 2 and 3.

Procedure:

Step I   Distribute copies of The Boundary Role Worksheet.

Ask participants to read the exercise and to answer the questions. *Allow 5 minutes.*

Step II   *Small group discussion*
Divide participants into groups of three or four persons for discussion.
Allow 15 minutes.

Step III   *Full group discussion*
Lead a discussion focusing on the following:

- Do you recognize the boundary role concept?

- What is its impact on your work and performance?

- How you deal with it?

Ask participants to share any personal experience that they have had. *Allow 15 minutes.*

Step IV   Summarize.

Note: If you wish to cover the Adams' Paradox material, move on to Boundary Roles Exercise 2: *The Adams' Paradox.*

WORKSHEET: The Boundary Role

Boundary role persons are responsible for interactions with people outside their organization in the acquisition and disposal of organizational resources and for the transfer of needed information across organizational boundaries. These persons not only occupy one of the most crucial positions within an organization, but also one of the highest potential conflict positions. They are subject both to the demands of the organization in which they are members and to the demands from the external systems with which they interact. Examples of boundary role positions include salespeople; buyers, who purchase goods from external parties; and government regulators.

Boundary role persons are in a unique position in that they are close to the external environment and have access to information unavailable to other organizational members. They are the organization's representatives to the outside and, generally, the organization's source of influence over the external environment. Because boundary role negotiations and external relations are so essential to an organization's functioning, the factors that have an effect on them need to be understood.

QUESTIONS

1. Does our department serve a boundary role function?

2. What demands are placed on us as boundary role people?

3. What is the impact of the above on our performance?

The Adams' Paradox

Objectives:	To discuss the Adams' Paradox and its impact
	To review the impact of the Adams' Paradox on the participants work
Time:	20–30 minutes
Group Size:	3–4
Materials:	Adams' Paradox Worksheet.
Trainer's Notes:	Ideally, this exercise should be run in conjunction with Boundary Role Exercise 1: *The Boundary Role*. The two exercises work well together. However, it is possible to conduct this exercise without the previous one.
Procedure:	The following procedure assumes that you have already conducted Boundary Roles Exercise 1.
Step I	Have participants remain in the same groups.
Step II	Distribute copies of The Adams' Paradox Worksheet. Have the groups discuss and answer questions at the bottom of the worksheet. Allow 10 to 15 minutes.
Step III	*Full group discussion* Lead a discussion that focuses on the worksheet questions. Pay particular attention to how participants can address the Adams' Paradox. *Allow 15 minutes.*
Note:	Encourage the group to identify how they can deal with the Adams' Paradox Issue.

WORKSHEET: The Adams' Paradox

The Adams' Paradox is named for the scholar J. S. Adams, who proposed that boundary role persons will be more likely to develop friendlier, more cooperative relations with external parties. This is done in an attempt to develop optimal, long-term agreements with outsiders, rather than maximal, short-term agreements. Friendly relations with outsiders enhance the referent power of the boundary role person, which is often the only source of power he or she has in regard to the relationship.

However, this cooperative, friendly behavior may cause internal constituents to question the boundary role person's loyalty and may lead them to monitor more closely this person's behavior, thereby restricting his or her autonomy. The increased monitoring may be seen by the boundary role person as distrust, and a sign that cooperative behavior is not valued. To prove their loyalty, boundary role persons will become more competitive in their negotiations and less friendly with external parties. The tougher stance may make them appear unreasonable, leading to less collaborative agreements and fewer successful negotiations with outsiders over the long term. It will diminish their referent power over the outsider.

In Adams' words (1976):

> "The paradox is noteworthy, for it suggests that a rewarding organizational climate may be self-destructive and may lead eventually to less organizational effectiveness in boundary transactions than might be supposed."

QUESTIONS

1. Is the Adams' Paradox an issue for us in our department? Please explain.

2. How does the Paradox show itself?

3. What steps can we take to address this issue?

Departmental Assessment

Objectives:	To assess the effectiveness of the participants' departments in dealing with outside groups
Time:	30 minutes
Group Size:	3–4
Materials:	Worksheet for each participant.
Trainer's Notes:	For maximum impact, this exercise should be used in conjunction with Boundary Roles Exercises 1 and 2.
	If you have conducted the previous exercises, keep participants in the same small groups.

Procedure:

Step I Distribute copies of the Departmental Assessment worksheet. Reach consensus on the departments and outside groups that should be identified in Questions 1 and 3.

Step II Ask participants to complete the worksheet on their own. *Allow 5 minutes.*

Step III *Small group discussion*
Divide participants into small groups to discuss the questions and reach consensus on the assessment ratings. *Allow 10 minutes.*

Step IV *Reporting Back—Allow 15 minutes.*
Ask for a reporting back.

Step V *Full group discussion*
Discuss each of the questions.

- Pay particular attention to those questions for which the rating is low.

- For these low-scoring questions, you should explore the impact on relationships and effectiveness in dealing with those departments or outside groups.

- Help the group focus on how to deal with the low-scoring department. Help them build a specific action plan.

WORKSHEET: Departmental Assessment

1. Overall, how would you evaluate your department's performance with other departments and outside groups?

Department: _____

Outside group: _____

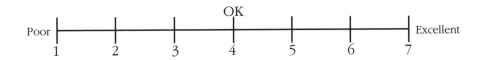

Why?

2. How would you describe the company's relationship with these groups?

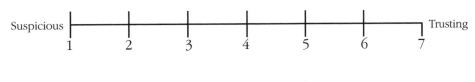

3. How do you thing the following departments would rate your department's effeciveness (Fill in the appropriate departments.)

Department: _____

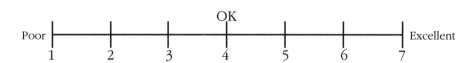

Department: _____

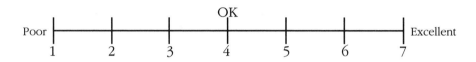

Department: _____

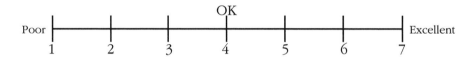

Department: _____

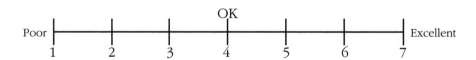

Department: _____

Notes:

Negotiation at Work: Maximize Your Team's Skills with 60 High-Impact Activities, ©2012 HRD Press.
Published by AMACOM Books, American Management Association, www.amanet.org.

XVI. Sales Negotiation

Success Factors*

Objectives:	To identify the factors critical to negotiation success and failure
Time:	Open
Group Size:	2–5
Materials:	Pre-work distributed prior to the program.
Trainer's Notes:	This exercise is ideal when used as a pre-work activity with salespeople. When used this way, it should be sent out at least one week prior to the program. Ask that Parts 1, 2, and 3 be completed prior to the program and brought to the first session.
	We suggest using this material early in the program so that it can provide a framework for the remainder of the workshop.
	If time is a significant issue, you can use this material without the small-group activity. Just have participants report back on Part 4.

Procedure:

Step I   Ask participants to pair up and share the pre-work with each other.

Indicate that they should spend most of their time on Parts 3 and 4. Tell them that they will be asked to share the results of their discussion with the rest of the group. *Allow 15 to 30 minutes.*

Step II   *Reporting Back*
Ask each group to report back on the items listed in Part 4. After all the groups have reported, check to ensure that all the items have been covered.

- Encourage discussion about each of the items and why it is seen as important.

- Summarize the list and relate the activity to the outline of your workshop.

*Contributed by Phil Faris Associates

PRE-WORK: Success Factors

Part 1

Describe a situation where a negotiation was particularly successful.

Account: _____

Contact(s): _____

Situation/Issues being negotiated: _____

_____

Your initial position: _____

_____

Their initial position: _____

_____

_____

The final results: _____

_____

Part 2

Describe a situation where the negotiation was not very successful.

Account: _____

Contact(s): _____

Situation/Issues being negotiated: _____

_____

Your initial position: _____

_____

Their initial position: _____

_____

_____

The final results: _____

_____

Part 3

What were the biggest differences between the two situations?

_____

_____

_____

_____

Part 4

In teams, identify the three most critical factors for a successful negotiation. Be prepared to share your responses with the group.

1.

_____

_____

_____

2.

_____

_____

_____

3.

_____

_____

_____

Notes on responses from other groups:

_____

_____

_____

_____

Negotiation at Work: Maximize Your Team's Skills with 60 High-Impact Activities, ©2012 HRD Press.
Published by AMACOM Books, American Management Association, www.amanet.org.

Sales Practices Assessment

Objective: The ultimate judge of a salesperson is the customer. Knowing how you are viewed by your customer is a critical first step toward improving your effectiveness. This activity is designed to help you assess your performance of the sales practices that customers say are most important to them.

Method:

1. Distribute the handout for the Sales Practices Assessment.

2. Explain that each sales practice is to be assessed from the participant customer's point of view. In effect, the assessment is asking participants to answer the question, "How do my customers view me?"

3. Have participants complete the assessment individually. This should take 10 minutes.

4. Have participants form pairs or triads to discuss the results. Everyone takes a turn in the "hot seat" and describes their results. Others ask for illustrations or examples and give feedback. Allow 30 minutes for this part of the activity.

5. Lead a discussion on ways participants can improve their sales practices.

Sales Practices Assessment

Directions

Using the scale below, rate each practice as you feel your customers would rate it.

RATING SCALE

4 – Strongly Agree

3 – Inclined to Agree

2 – Inclined to Disagree

1 – Strongly Disagree

KNOWLEDGE   **RATING**

This is a salesperson who…

• Understands business issues and economic trends that impact business	1	2	3	4
• Knows the competition	1	2	3	4
• Understands the decision-making process in our company	1	2	3	4
• Demonstrates knowledge about his/her product and presents it in a manner that is easy for me to understand	1	2	3	4
• Understands my goals and helps me achieve them	1	2	3	4
• Uses the knowledge of our business and company to develop better ways of doing business	1	2	3	4

MANAGING RELATIONSHIPS

This is a salesperson who…

• Is enjoyable to work with	1	2	3	4
• Is truthful and honest with me	1	2	3	4
• Demonstrates his/her desire to do business with me	1	2	3	4
• Listens and understands my situation and concerns	1	2	3	4
• Responds responsibly to my pricing and budget needs	1	2	3	4
• Is accessible when I need him/her	1	2	3	4
• Makes and keeps commitments	1	2	3	4
• Feels confident and comfortable working with others	1	2	3	4
• Takes a long-term approach to doing business with me	1	2	3	4

(continued)

RATING SCALE

4 – Strongly Agree

3 – Inclined to Agree

2 – Inclined to Disagree

1 – Strongly Disagree

MANAGING THE SALES PROCESS

This is a salesperson who...

	RATING			
Presents self in a positive and professional manner	1	2	3	4
Helps me solve problems and meets my needs in an emergency	1	2	3	4
Effectively gets his/her company to respond to our requests	1	2	3	4
Makes creative solutions to improve our company's business problems	1	2	3	4
Finds ways for my company to provide a better product or service to our customers	1	2	3	4
Takes personal responsibility throughout the entire sales process	1	2	3	4
Alerts me of changes or problems that can affect me	1	2	3	4
Makes it easy to do business with his/her company	1	2	3	4
Thoroughly responds to my requests and concerns	1	2	3	4
Effectively uses his/her company's resources to meet my needs	1	2	3	4

Negotiation at Work: Maximize Your Team's Skills with 60 High-Impact Activities, ©2012 HRD Press.
Published by AMACOM Books, American Management Association, www.amanet.org.

Features, Advantages, Benefits, Proof

Objectives:
- To demonstrate the relationship between features, advantages, and benefits of a product/service

- To develop a better understanding of the features, advantages, and benefits of a product/service

- To identify sources to prove benefit statements about a product/service

Method:
1. Lead a brief discussion on features, advantages, and benefits. Make sure the group understands the following definitions:

   a) Features are anything attached to, or descriptive of, the physical make-up of a product or service.

   b) Advantages described what the feature does that is unique.

   c) Benefits are the intangible mental concepts or physical results that the features and their advantages provide the customer. Benefits answer the question all customers ask or expect to have answered for them every time they approach a buying decision (e.g., "What's in it for me?").

   Discuss the need to provide clients with proof of product claims.

2. Divide the group into four teams.

3. Distribute the handout to each team and assign each team a specific product or service. Each team is to identify six features for their assigned product. *Allow 5 minutes.*

4. Have each team pass their handout to the team to their right.

5. Working with the six features provided by the other team, tell teams to develop a list of advantages for each feature. Instruct the teams to be creative. *Allow 10 minutes.*

6. Again, have teams pass their handouts to the team to their right.

7. Have teams develop as many benefits as possible for each of the advantages provided for them by the other teams. *Allow 10 minutes.*

8. Have teams pass their handouts one more time to the team to their right.

9. Have teams develop at least one proof source for each benefit listed on their handouts. *Allow 10 minutes.*

10. Tell teams to prepare a presentation using the information contained on the completed handout. *Allow 10 minutes to prepare and 5 minutes for each presentation.*

11. Have each team make their presentation. Allow a question-and-answer period after each presentation.

12. Conclude the activity with a brief discussion on how to apply what was learned on the job.

Notes and Variations:

1. Collect the completed worksheets and have them typed. Then distribute them to all participants for a product review.

2. To increase competition, award prizes for teams that develop the most benefits or the most creative proof source, etc.

Features, Advantages, Benefits, Proof

Product/Service: _____

Features	Advantages	Benefits	Proof

The Approach Piece

Objectives: Sometimes the hardest task you will face is getting in the door to tell your sales story. Getting the attention of decision makers and whetting their appetite for what you have to present is an important first step in the sales process. The Approach Piece is designed to help you accomplish this first step. This activity helps participants to do the following:

- Develop an approach piece.

- Receive feedback on how to improve their approach piece.

- Exchange ideas about approach pieces with other participants.

Method: 1. Distribute An Approach Piece Assignment and have participants read it.

2. Briefly discuss the handout's contents.

3. Assign to participants the task of developing their own approach pieces for the next meeting. Each participant should develop one approach piece.

Note: Since research and hard work is usually required, this activity is done best when adequate time is allowed for development and creativity.

4. Have each participant present his/her approach piece, with a feedback session immediately following.

5. Lead a discussion from the Discussion Questions handout.

An Approach Piece Assignment

Directions

Develop an approach piece and be prepared to present it at the next meeting.

Guidelines

1. Read the Approach Piece Overview below.
2. Review existing sales literature, marketing materials, trade magazines, etc.
3. If necessary, consult other salespeople.
4. Develop your approach piece and bring it with you to the next meeting.

Approach Piece Overview

The initial contact is a key step in the sales process. It is this step that sets the groundwork for the rest of the sales process. A poor call on the initial contact greatly reduces the chances of closing the sale.

The objectives of the initial contact call are to:

- Make the prospect aware of his/her needs (problems)
- Arouse the prospect's interest in having those needs satisfied
- Show how you may be able to solve those needs

The perfect tool to help you accomplish these objectives is an approach piece. An approach piece is a sales tool that gives you:

- A visual aid to focus the prospect's attention and stimulate their interest
- A foundation from which to build your sales message
- A conceptual track to run on to ensure that all points are covered
- A professional image that helps you make your point and move the sales process forward

An effective approach piece should be brief, make an impact, and contain the following:

- Material that makes a general benefit statement and that helps you develop the prospect's interest. This can include the following:
  — Newspaper or magazine articles
  — Product sheets
  — Anything that will help you generate interest

(continued)

- Proof statements. These are materials that clarify strengths and reduce skepticism, including the following:
    — Testimonial letters
    — Advertisement
    — Promotional material

The Approach Piece: Discussion Questions

1. What are the advantages of an approach piece?

_____

_____

_____

_____

_____

_____

_____

_____

2. What are the potential problems of using an approach piece?

_____

_____

_____

_____

_____

_____

_____

3. In what ways can you make your approach piece more effective?

_____

_____

_____

_____

_____

_____

_____

Product Knowledge Jeopardy

Objective: To increase participants' understanding of their products/services

Method:

1. Divide participants into teams of four to six, with one participant in each team becoming the captain.

2. Distribute the worksheet and ask teams to develop 20 product knowledge questions and answers by using the format of the Jeopardy game show. *Allow 20 minutes.*

3. When teams have developed their lists of questions and answers, review the rules of the game on the handout for the rules.

4. Answer participant questions.

5. Choose a number from 1 to 10. Then have the captain from each team try to guess what it is. The captain who comes closest to guessing the number starts the game.

6. Play to a certain point total or for a fixed period of time (e.g., 30 minutes).

7. Tally results and announce the winner.

WORKSHEET: Product Knowledge Jeopardy

Directions

As a team, develop 20 product knowledge questions and answers by using the format of the game show Jeopardy.

Example:

The **answer** is: The **question** is:

    16 ounces   *What is our most popular sized container?*

	ANSWER	CORRECT QUESTION
1.		
2.		
3.		
4.		
5.		
6.		
7.		
8.		
9.		
10.		
11.		
12.		
13.		
14.		
15.		
16.		
17.		
18.		
19.		
20.		

Product Knowledge Jeopardy Rules

1. The game begins with an assigned team reading one of their answers.

2. Other teams may respond by raising their hands.

3. The first person to raise a hand may respond to the answer. The team giving the answer determines who raised a hand first.

4. To score points, a representative for the team must respond correctly to the answer provided, putting the response in the form of a question. A correct response earns a team 10 points.

5. If the first team fails to provide the correct response, other teams may volunteer to respond by raising their hands.

6. A correct response by the second or any subsequent volunteer is worth 5 team points.

7. If no team can provide the correct response, the team providing the answer is awarded 5 points.

8. The team that correctly responds must read one of their answers to the other teams.

9. Any disputes are resolved by the facilitator.

Give It to Me . . . I Want It!

Objectives: Selling is a dynamic process between a buyer and a seller. This exercise is designed to help participants understand the process from both the seller's perspective and the buyer's perspective. Specifically, the exercise will help participants:

- Recognize the basic elements of the selling/buying process

- Identify how salespeople influence the buying decision

- Identify how buyers influence the selling process

Method:

1. Distribute the handout and review the rules of the exercise.

2. Explain the seller's role by stating that his/her goal is to get business ("it") from the buyer. However, the only way a seller can get the business is to ask, "Give it to me. . .I want it!" The seller can make this demand as often as he/she likes and with any inflection desired, but those are the only words the seller can use.

3. Explain the buyer's role by stating that his/her goal is to buy what the seller is selling. If the buyer really feels the seller wants the business ("it"), the buyer can give it by saying, "Yes, you can have it." However, if the buyer doesn't really feel the seller wants the business, he/she must say, "No, you can't have it." These are the only two statements the buyer is allowed to use.

4. Explain how roles change. The group is organized in a single file, facing in the same direction. The seller is the person who is at one end of the line and turns to face the next person in line. Once the seller gets "it," he/she goes to the end of the line and waits for his/her turn to be the buyer. The buyer now becomes the seller by facing the next person in line, who in turn becomes the buyer. This process continues until everyone has been both a seller and a buyer.

5. Before starting, make sure everyone understands the rules, and remind the group that they will get the most out of the exercise if everyone "plays the game."

6. Conduct the exercise. Make sure participants follow the rules while playing the game.

7. Participants individually reflect on the exercise by completing the discussion questions on the second handout.

8. Conduct a discussion of the exercise by reviewing the participants' answers to the discussion questions. Possible responses are listed below:

- Why did you get it? Responses may include:

    — I wanted it.

    — I was sincere

    — I made eye contact.

    — I was persistent.

    — I changed my approach.

- Why did you give it? Responses may include:

    — I got tired of saying "no."

    — I thought the seller really wanted it.

    — The seller asked me the way I wanted him/her to ask.

- Who had control, the buyer or the seller? Why? Responses may include:

    — The buyer did, because he/she decided when and if the seller would get it.

    — The seller did, because he/she controlled how the buyer was asked.

- How did control change as the exercise progressed? Responses may include:

    — The longer the seller asked for it, the more difficult it became for the buyer to say no.

- What did you learn about selling from this exercise? Responses may include:

    — You have to ask for the business to get it.

    — You have to get past "no" to make a sale.

    — Buyer's hold the key to how you must ask for the business.

    — If you meet a buyer's buying criteria, you get the sale.

    — Persistence can be a powerful tool.

    — If we feel the buyer must give it to us, we have more confidence in pursuing the business.

- What did you learn about yourself from this exercise? Responses may include:

  — I didn't like being the buyer.

  — I liked being in control as the buyer.

  — I found it hard to keep asking for it.

  — I wanted the seller to change, and when he didn't, I didn't want to give it to him.

Notes and Variations:

1. If the group has ten or more participants, break them into two lines and run the exercise simultaneously. A good rule of thumb is to keep the lines to at least five, and to no more than nine.

2. People may feel a little awkward at first. Draw this out in the discussion and relate it back to actual sales situations. For example, most people feel a little awkward when they sell with an audience, such as a boss or product manager.

Give It to Me . . . I Want It!

Directions

You are about to participate in an exercise with other members of the class. The rules for this exercise are simple and few, but they must be adhered to precisely at all times.

Rules

1. Each person will have the opportunity to be both a seller and a buyer. The seller's goal is to get business ("it") from the buyer.

2. When you are a seller, you must say to the buyer, "Give it to me. . .I want it!" You may make this statement any way you want and as many times as you want, until the buyer says, "Okay, you can have it."

3. When you are the buyer, you must not give "it" unless you feel the seller really wants it. If you feel the seller really wants it, you can give it to him/her by saying, "Okay, you can have it." If you don't feel the seller really wants it, then say, "No, you can't have it, you're not ready yet."

4. The only words that can be spoken by either the seller or the buyer are the ones mentioned above.

DISCUSSION QUESTIONS: Give It to Me . . . I Want It!

Discussion Questions

1. Why did you get it?

_____

_____

_____

_____

2. Why did you give it?

_____

_____

_____

_____

3. Who had control, the buyer or the seller? Why?

_____

_____

_____

_____

4. What did you learn about selling from this exercise?

_____

_____

_____

_____

5. What did you learn about yourself from this exercise?

_____

_____

_____

_____

What Does It Take to Be a World-Class Salesperson?

Objectives:

- To help participants develop a practical model of a world-class salesperson

- To help participants assess themselves against the model and identify their strengths and improvement opportunities

Method:

1. Distribute the first worksheet (What Does It Take . . .) and ask participants to describe both the worst and best salesperson they have encountered as a consumer. Allow five minutes for individuals to complete descriptions.

2. Starting with the Worst Salesperson section, lead a discussion based on the group's responses. You should help participants focus on what the salesperson did that most influenced their assessment. Also, ask if participants remember the salesperson's name. **Note:** Most participants will remember the name of the best salesperson, but not the worst.

3. Lead a brief discussion of what a world-class salesperson is (e.g., the best of the best). Salespeople should use this as a model for assessing their own capabilities.

4. Distribute the second worksheet (World-Class Salesperson) and instruct participants to complete Part I individually. Allow five minutes.

5. Break participants into subgroups of four to eight and ask them to complete Part II of Handout 5.2. Remind groups to prioritize their list of characteristics. Allow the groups 20 minutes to compile their lists.

6. Develop a master list on a flip chart. Start the process by asking each group to give their top three characteristics. Then rotate from group to group until all the characteristics are listed.

7. Distribute the survey and instruct participants to copy the list of characteristics in the space provided and to assess themselves by circling the appropriate number on the scale from 1 to 10. Remind the group that a standard for a 10 is a world-class salesperson.

8. When the participants have completed their assessment, ask them to connect the circled numbers with straight lines. This accentuates both their strengths (peaks) and improvement opportunities (valleys).

Notes and Variations:

1. If there is an existing model or list of characteristics specific to the organization and these characteristics are not identified by any of the groups, add them to the final list.

2. This exercise can be used to establish a new higher standard of performance for salespeople.

3. This exercise can also be used as part of a development review process.

WORKSHEET: What Does It Take to Be a World-Class Salesperson?

Directions

We are all consumers. Therefore, we experience the satisfaction and frustration of dealing with salespeople. Think back to your past purchases and describe both the best and worst salesperson.

Worst Salesperson

Product or service: _____

Salesperson's name: _____

How do you feel about what you purchased?

_____

_____

_____

_____

_____

How do you feel about the salesperson?

_____

_____

_____

_____

_____

What did the salesperson do to cause you to feel as you do?

_____

_____

_____

_____

_____

(continued)

Best Salesperson

Product or service: _____

Salesperson's name: _____

How do you feel about what you purchased?

_____

_____

_____

_____

_____

How do you feel about the salesperson?

_____

_____

_____

_____

_____

What did the salesperson do to cause you to feel as you do?

_____

_____

_____

_____

_____

Negotiation at Work: Maximize Your Team's Skills with 60 High-Impact Activities, ©2012 HRD Press.
Published by AMACOM Books, American Management Association, www.amanet.org.

WORKSHEET: World-Class Salesperson

Part I

Individually, list the characteristics you feel contribute most to the success of a world-class salesperson.

_____

_____

_____

_____

_____

_____

_____

_____

_____

_____

Part II

In your group, develop a composite list of world-class salesperson characteristics in prioritized order.

_____

_____

_____

_____

_____

_____

_____

_____

_____

_____

_____

Salesperson's Personal Survey

Directions

1. In the space provided, write the final list of characteristics.
2. Assess the extent each characteristic describes you and circle the appropriate number.

Rating Scale

Not Descriptive   **1   2   3   4   5   6   7   8   9   10**   Very Descriptive

Characteristics	Your Assessment
1.	1 2 3 4 5 6 7 8 9 10
2.	1 2 3 4 5 6 7 8 9 10
3.	1 2 3 4 5 6 7 8 9 10
4.	1 2 3 4 5 6 7 8 9 10
5.	1 2 3 4 5 6 7 8 9 10
6.	1 2 3 4 5 6 7 8 9 10
7.	1 2 3 4 5 6 7 8 9 10
8.	1 2 3 4 5 6 7 8 9 10
9.	1 2 3 4 5 6 7 8 9 10
10.	1 2 3 4 5 6 7 8 9 10
11.	1 2 3 4 5 6 7 8 9 10
12.	1 2 3 4 5 6 7 8 9 10
13.	1 2 3 4 5 6 7 8 9 10
14.	1 2 3 4 5 6 7 8 9 10
15.	1 2 3 4 5 6 7 8 9 10
16.	1 2 3 4 5 6 7 8 9 10

The Sales Presentation Role Play

Objectives:
- To help participants try new sales skills without risk of failure

- To give participants feedback on the effect of their behavior on others

- To improve participants' effectiveness in delivering an effective sales presentation

- To improve participants' ability to recognize effective and ineffective behaviors in themselves and in others

- To share and refine successful skills techniques

Method:
1. Have participants break into teams of three.

2. Distribute the first two handouts of Exercise 8 on role play. Review the objectives, guidelines, and time frame for the activity. Properly position the activity by explaining each person's role and by clarifying the group's expectations for the activity.

3. Have the teams conduct their role plays.

4. When the role-playing period is over, lead a group discussion based on the Discussion Questions in the last handout.

Notes and Variations:
1. To assist the participants in giving effective feedback, suggest that they use the following procedure:

   - The seller goes first. He/she must assess his/her own performance against the established objectives or criteria. The seller must start with positives and then move to improvement opportunities.

   - The buyer goes second, describing his/her objectives and needs and explaining why he/she did or did not buy.

   - Finally, the observer gives his/her feedback by starting with the positives and then moving to the improvement opportunities.

2. At the start of the role-play period, move around to each team to help them get started.

3. During the role-play period, keep teams on track by telling them how much time is available.

4. Allow observers to use a general feedback sheet or a specific feedback sheet or to develop their own.

Group Role-Play Guidelines

Directions

In this exercise you will apply your understanding of an actual sales situation to a role-play situation in order to develop the best possible strategy to improve the situation and/or make the sale. You will work in teams and provide feedback to each other. The method and procedure is as follows:

1. **Select Team**
   - Form a team of three people. Choose people who you believe can assist you in the task as outlined below.

2. **Individual Preparation** (for each person who will be playing the seller's role)
   - Fill out the role-play objectives sheet to determine what skills you want to improve.
   - Select a situation about which you will do a role play. One other member of your team will play the part of the buyer.
   - Complete and discuss with the buyer the Role Play Information Sheet handout. This will give your buyer some background information and allow him/her to do a more realistic job.
   - Determine your sales objectives for the role-play meeting from your point of view. Again, focus on the two or three key points you think need to be discussed.
   - Plan a strategy for the meeting:
     — What research will you need?
     — What objections do you anticipate?
     — How will you present the information?
     — What questions will you ask?
   - For observers: Use the handouts or make up an observer's sheet that will allow you to take notes and provide the seller with specific feedback in the skill areas he or she is trying to improve.
   - For buyers: While the seller is planning his/her strategy, you should plan yours. Become familiar with the facts, plan your objections, and determine your "hot buttons" based on the information from the seller. Be as realistic as you can. Don't "overplay" the role, but also don't be a pushover.

3. **Teamwork**
   - Team members will alternate three roles: (1) buyer, (2) seller, and (3) observer.

Each role play should "begin" at the point the seller chooses so that he/she can get the most practice. The salesperson should make the observer and buyer aware of his/her sales objective and the skills he or she would like feedback on. The role play should last 10 minutes. After this role play, there should be a period of feedback from the "buyer" and "observer." The seller should then try again, using any feedback he/she chooses. The sequences are as follows:

- Setup and instructions: 5 minutes
- Role play: 10 minutes
- Feedback: 5 minutes
- Re-do: 10 minutes

Each role-play sequence should take approximately 30 minutes. The groups' work should last no more than 90 minutes.

Role-Play Learning Objectives

The purpose of this role play is to help you work on those situations and behaviors that are the most difficult for you. Before you begin the individual work, decide what you want to work on (i.e., What skills do you want to improve?). Use the items below to help you decide:

Self-Assessment: The most difficult thing for me to do in a sales situation is:

_____

_____

_____

Situation Assessment: The most difficult type of buyer for me is:

_____

_____

_____

Objectives: What I want to work on (and get feedback about) is:

_____

_____

_____

Negotiation at Work: Maximize Your Team's Skills with 60 High-Impact Activities, ©2012 HRD Press.
Published by AMACOM Books, American Management Association, www.amanet.org.

WORKSHEET: Role-Play Information

(To be completed by seller and given to person who will role-play buyer's part)

1. Buyer's name: _____

2. Buyer's background: _____

    Age range: _____

    Family situation: _____

3. Account history: _____
_____
_____
_____

4. Behavioral style/personality: _____
_____
_____

5. Business needs and goals: _____
_____
_____

6. Personal needs and goals: _____
_____
_____

7. Objectives for the call: _____
_____
_____

8. Objections (to be completed by the person who will role play the buyer):
_____
_____

WORKSHEET: Observer Feedback (General)

Buyer's name:_____

Your role is to provide feedback to the seller on two dimensions:

a) **In what areas does the seller want feedback?** You should ask him/her this question during the setup period prior to the role play. This feedback can be positive and/or negative.

b) **Any other areas you see** in which the seller could improve his/her effectiveness—or is already doing an effective job.

Seller wants feedback about...	Other observations

WORKSHEET: Observer Feedback (Specific)

Name of seller: _____

PRESENTATION

Did he/she establish rapport/trust? ❏ Yes ❏ No

How? _____

_____

_____

Did he/she identify the buyer's problem or goal? ❏ Yes ❏ No

How? _____

_____

_____

Did he/she position benefits as a solution to the problem or goal? ❏ Yes ❏ No

Give examples: _____

_____

_____

Did he/she answer the buyer's objections? ❏ Yes ❏ No

Which ones? _____

_____

_____

How were they answered? _____

_____

_____

Did he/she adapt the presentation to the personal and business
needs of the buyer?   ❑ Yes   ❑ No

Give examples: _____

_____

_____

Did he/she ask for a commitment to action?   ❑ Yes   ❑ No

Describe (how many and what questions used): _____

_____

_____

PRESENTATION MANNER

Initial Impact

Attention obtained at start?   ❑ Yes   ❑ No

Comments: _____

_____

_____

Posture?   ❑ Good   ❑ Fair   ❑ Distracting

How? _____

_____

_____

Eye Contact

Made initial contact?   ❑ Yes   ❑ No

Maintained contact?   ❑ Yes   ❑ No

Comments: _____

_____

_____

Negotiation at Work: Maximize Your Team's Skills with 60 High-Impact Activities, ©2012 HRD Press.
Published by AMACOM Books, American Management Association, www.amanet.org.

Hands

Used hands to support spoken word?   ❏ Yes   ❏ No

Comments: _____

_____

_____

Voice

Good impact?   ❏ Yes   ❏ No

Proper volume?   ❏ Yes   ❏ No

Meaningful language?   ❏ Yes   ❏ No

Enthusiastic?   ❏ Yes   ❏ No

Speed?   ❏ Too fast   ❏ Too slow   ❏ Appropriate

Comments: _____

_____

_____

Organization

Appear prepared?   ❏ Yes   ❏ No

Smooth flowing?   ❏ Yes   ❏ No

Comments: _____

_____

_____

Sales Aids

Used sales aids?   ❏ Yes   ❏ No

Used well?   ❏ Yes   ❏ No

Kept control of aids?   ❏ Yes   ❏ No

Comments: _____

_____

_____

Sales Presentation Role Play: Discussion Questions

1. What did you learn as the seller?

_____

_____

_____

_____

_____

2. What did you learn as the buyer?

_____

_____

_____

_____

_____

3. What did you learn as the observer?

_____

_____

_____

_____

_____

4. What skills do you want to practice more?

_____

_____

_____

_____

_____

Selling Skills Inventory

Objectives:
- To provide a structure for assessing selling skills

- To help salespeople identify their selling skills strengths and improvement opportunities

Method:
1. Distribute the worksheet for Selling Knowledge and Skills Inventory and the Selling Skills Inventory Analysis handout.

2. Have participants individually complete the inventory and Strengths and Improvement Opportunities sections of the analysis. *Allow about 15 minutes.*

3. Pairs or triads meet to discuss the results. Each participant takes a turn in the "hot seat" and describes the results of his/her inventory and analysis. Others in the group ask questions to clarify the analysis and give feedback. Allow 45 minutes for this process.

4. The Building on My Strengths and Actions for Improving sections in the second handout are completed individually. Allow about 10 minutes.

Notes and Variations:
1. Sales managers may want to complete a copy of the inventory for each salesperson and use it as a basis for a developmental review.

2. Sales managers may want to use the group's results from the inventory for the basis of a sales training needs analysis.

WORKSHEET: Selling Knowledge and Skills Inventory

Directions

This inventory helps you assess your own selling knowledge and skill and then identify your strength and improvement opportunities. Answer each question as honestly as you can.

1. As you go through the inventory, put a checkmark (✓) in the appropriate column.

2. Fill in the blank spaces with any additional skills that are important for you.

3. Go back over the list and circle three or four items from the whole list that you feel are your biggest strengths at this time. Write these strengths in the space provided on the analysis sheet.

4. Next, go back over the list and circle three or four items from the whole list that you feel would be most useful to improve at this time. Write these improvement opportunities in the space provided on the analysis sheet.

5. Discuss your results with another person.

6. Complete the Building on My Strengths and Actions for Improving sections on the analysis sheet.

(continued)

KNOWLEDGE

Customer Knowledge	Needs Much Improvement	Needs Some Improvement	Needs No Improvement
How knowledgeable are you about your customer's…			
• Business?	❑	❑	❑
• Needs and uses of your products/services?			
• Buying patterns (including when they buy, who is involved, why)?	❑	❑	❑
• Personal needs?	❑	❑	❑
• Professional needs?	❑	❑	❑
• Attitude toward you and your products/services?	❑	❑	❑
• Other: _____	❑	❑	❑

Product Knowledge	Needs Much Improvement	Needs Some Improvement	Needs No Improvement
How knowledgeable are you about…			
• How your product is made or service is delivered?	❑	❑	❑
• How your product impacts your customer's business?	❑	❑	❑
• How your products/services compare to the competition's?	❑	❑	❑
• Other: _____	❑	❑	❑

Market/Industry Knowledge	Needs Much Improvement	Needs Some Improvement	Needs No Improvement
How knowledgeable are you about…			
• Market conditions that impact your customers and your business?	❑	❑	❑
• Industry factors or trends that impact your business?	❑	❑	❑
• Other: _____	❑	❑	❑

(*continued*)

Competitive Knowledge	Needs Much Improvement	Needs Some Improvement	Needs No Improvement
How knowledgeable are you about...			
• Who your competitors are?	❑	❑	❑
• What your competitors' strengths and weaknesses are?	❑	❑	❑
• How your customers view your competitors?	❑	❑	❑
• How your competitors market and sell their products/services?	❑	❑	❑
• Other: _____	❑	❑	❑

Self-Knowledge	Needs Much Improvement	Needs Some Improvement	Needs No Improvement
How knowledgeable are you about...			
• How you interact with others?	❑	❑	❑
• Your selling skills strengths and improvement opportunities?	❑	❑	❑
• How your customers perceive you?	❑	❑	❑
• Other: _____	❑	❑	❑

(continued)

SKILLS

Developing New Business	Needs Much Improvement	Needs Some Improvement	Needs No Improvement
How effective are you at...			
• Analyzing the potential of your territory?	❏	❏	❏
• Identifying and qualifying potential customers?	❏	❏	❏
• Generating qualified leads?	❏	❏	❏
• Gaining information about prospects and their businesses?	❏	❏	❏
• Using the telephone to get appointments with decision makers?	❏	❏	❏
• Developing compelling business reasons for each customer contact?	❏	❏	❏
• Obtaining references and referrals?	❏	❏	❏
• Other: _____	❏	❏	❏

Discovering Needs	Needs Much Improvement	Needs Some Improvement	Needs No Improvement
How effective are you at...			
• Responding to the customer's buying process?	❏	❏	❏
• Observing during sales calls?	❏	❏	❏
• Listening for understanding?	❏	❏	❏
• Using open and closed questions to get appropriate information from the customer?	❏	❏	❏
• Discovering and responding to recognized and unrecognized needs?	❏	❏	❏
• Other: _____	❏	❏	❏

(continued)

Negotiation at Work: Maximize Your Team's Skills with 60 High-Impact Activities, ©2012 HRD Press.
Published by AMACOM Books, American Management Association, www.amanet.org.

Presenting	Needs Much Improvement	Needs Some Improvement	Needs No Improvement

How effective are you at...

	Needs Much Improvement	Needs Some Improvement	Needs No Improvement
• Identifying how to use your product or service to satisfy customers' needs?	❑	❑	❑
• Setting specific and measurable call objectives?	❑	❑	❑
• Preparing for each sales call?	❑	❑	❑
• Influencing buyers?	❑	❑	❑
• Personalizing the presentations?	❑	❑	❑
• Building urgency and relevance into presentations?	❑	❑	❑
• Differentiating and targeting benefits?	❑	❑	❑
• Assessing where the buyer is throughout the sales call?	❑	❑	❑
• Using visual aids?	❑	❑	❑
• Evaluating each sales call?	❑	❑	❑
• Communicating clearly in writing?	❑	❑	❑
• Other: _____	❑	❑	❑

Neutralizing and Resolving Objections	Needs Much Improvement	Needs Some Improvement	Needs No Improvement

How effective are you at...

	Needs Much Improvement	Needs Some Improvement	Needs No Improvement
• Understanding how objections contribute to the selling process?	❑	❑	❑
• Neutralizing (or pre-answering) objections during the presentation?	❑	❑	❑
• Recognizing the nature and origin of an objection?	❑	❑	❑
• Using objections to gain sales momentum?	❑	❑	❑
• Responding to the most common objections?	❑	❑	❑
• Other: _____	❑	❑	❑

(continued)

Closing	Needs Much Improvement	Needs Some Improvement	Needs No Improvement
How effective are you at…			
• Using empathy and leadership to gain commitments?	❑	❑	❑
• Recognizing and responding to body language and buying signals?	❑	❑	❑
• Using trial closes and tie-downs to manage the commitment process?	❑	❑	❑
• Developing closing strategies?	❑	❑	❑
• Formulating closes appropriate to the buyer's needs?	❑	❑	❑
• Other: _____	❑	❑	❑

Negotiating	Needs Much Improvement	Needs Some Improvement	Needs No Improvement
How effective are you at…			
• Recognizing when to negotiate?	❑	❑	❑
• Adapting your negotiating style?	❑	❑	❑
• Developing "currencies" to increase your bargaining power?	❑	❑	❑
• Developing a negotiating plan?	❑	❑	❑
• Making concessions effectively?	❑	❑	❑
• Building trust during the negotiating?	❑	❑	❑
• Other: _____	❑	❑	❑

(*continued*)

Negotiation at Work: Maximize Your Team's Skills with 60 High-Impact Activities, ©2012 HRD Press.
Published by AMACOM Books, American Management Association, www.amanet.org.

Developing and Managing Sales Relationships	Needs Much Improvement	Needs Some Improvement	Needs No Improvement
How effective are you at…			
• Identifying the personal needs of your buyers?	❏	❏	❏
• Identifying your natural selling approach?	❏	❏	❏
• Modifying your sales strategies to meet your buyer's needs and accomplish your objectives?	❏	❏	❏
• Other: _____	❏	❏	❏

Account Retention	Needs Much Improvement	Needs Some Improvement	Needs No Improvement
How effective are you at…			
• Recognizing the economic value of your customer?	❏	❏	❏
• Analyzing potential of existing accounts?	❏	❏	❏
• Establishing appropriate expectations for your product/ service?	❏	❏	❏
• Ensuring customer satisfaction when the product arrives or service begins?	❏	❏	❏
• Handling customer complaints?	❏	❏	❏
• Retaining customers in a competitive environment?	❏	❏	❏
• Enhancing customer loyalty with account servicing?	❏	❏	❏
• Creatively solving customer problems?	❏	❏	❏
• Working as part of a team to ensure customer satisfaction?	❏	❏	❏
• Other: _____	❏	❏	❏

(continued)

Mastering Your Time	Needs Much Improvement	Needs Some Improvement	Needs No Improvement
How effective are you at…			
• Determining the real value of your time?	❏	❏	❏
• Knowing where your time is spent?	❏	❏	❏
• Identifying time wasters?	❏	❏	❏
• Establishing priorities?	❏	❏	❏
• Using systems to improve your productivity?	❏	❏	❏
• Other: _____	❏	❏	❏

Managing Success	Needs Much Improvement	Needs Some Improvement	Needs No Improvement
How effective are you at…			
• Assessing what you need to do to become a world-class salesperson?	❏	❏	❏
• Dressing for success inside (mentally) and outside (physically)?	❏	❏	❏
• Analyzing sales activities?	❏	❏	❏
• Setting performance goals?	❏	❏	❏
• Managing yourself out of a slump?	❏	❏	❏
• Setting and achieving personal goals?	❏	❏	❏
• Other: _____	❏	❏	❏

List areas in which you would like additional training:

_____

_____

_____

_____

_____

_____

Negotiation at Work: Maximize Your Team's Skills with 60 High-Impact Activities, ©2012 HRD Press.
Published by AMACOM Books, American Management Association, www.amanet.org.

WORKSHEET: Selling Skills Inventory Analysis

Part I: Strengths

Go over the list in the inventory and circle three or four items that you feel are your biggest strengths at this time. Write these in the spaces below. After you have discussed your inventory results with someone else, record practical actions you can take for building on your strengths.

STRENGTHS	BUILDING ON MY STRENGTHS
1.	
2.	
3.	
4.	

Part II: Improvement Opportunities

Go over the list in the inventory again and circle three or four items that you would be most useful for you to improve at this time. Write these in the spaces below. After you have discussed your inventory results with someone else, record practical actions you can take for improving your skills.

IMPROVEMENT OPPORTUNITIES	ACTIONS FOR IMPROVING
1.	
2.	
3.	
4.	

Peer Group Review

Objectives:
- To help salespeople give and receive performance-based feedback

- To help participants establish realistic goals and to develop plans for achieving them

- To help salespeople identify the resources they need to achieve their goals

Method:
1. Put participants in peer groups of three or six (e.g., salespeople with similar experience, accounts, or needs).

2. Distribute Peer Group Review Planning Guide and Principles of Feedback.

3. During the peer group review, have participants make presentations to the group. The presentation should include the following:

   - Progress on your performance goals (this step is skipped on the initial meeting)

   - Establishing and committing to at least one goal for the next week

   - Outlining the actions that are planned to accomplish the goal(s)

   - Describing resources (including people) needed to help accomplish the goal(s)

4. After each presentation, other group members offer feedback and suggestions for helping their peers achieve their goals.

5. The peer group must adhere to the following rules:

   - Everyone makes a presentation.

   - Group members can ask questions to clarify points, offer their opinion, or give feedback, as long as they follow the established rules of feedback.

   - The presenter cannot defend his/her position. He/she can answer questions or ask questions to clarify a point made by the peer group.

6. The peer group is expected to schedule and to reinforce the rules.

WORKSHEET: Peer Group Review Planning Guide

My goals were _____

_____

_____

_____

I accomplished _____

_____

_____

_____

The reasons for my success/failure are _____

_____

_____

_____

My goals next week are _____

_____

_____

_____

I plan to accomplish this by doing _____

_____

_____

_____

To accomplish my goals, I will need assistance from _____

_____

_____

_____

Principles of Feedback

1. Feedback is descriptive rather than valuative. Because it presents a description of the feedback giver's personal reactions, it leaves the individual who is receiving the feedback free to use it or not to use it as he or she sees fit. By avoiding valuative language, it reduces the need for the individual to react defensively.

2. Feedback is specific rather than general. To be told that one is "dominating" will probably not be as useful as to be told that "just now when we were deciding the issue you did not listen to what others said and I felt forced to accept your arguments or face attack from you."

3. Feedback takes into account the needs of both the receiver and giver of feedback. Feedback can be destructive when it serves only our own needs and fails to consider the needs of the person on the receiving end.

4. Feedback is directed toward behavior that the receiver can do something about. Frustration is only increased when a person is reminded of some shortcoming over which he or she has no control.

5. Feedback is solicited rather than imposed. Feedback is most useful when the receiver has formulated the kind of questions that those who are observing the receiver can answer.

6. Feedback is well timed. In general, feedback is most useful at the earliest opportunity after the given behavior (depending, of course, on the person's readiness to hear it, on the support available from others, etc.).

7. Feedback is checked to ensure clear communications. One way of doing this is to have the receiver try to rephrase the feedback received to see if it corresponds to what the sender had in mind.

8. When feedback is given, both giver and receiver have the opportunity to check with others in the group the accuracy of the feedback. Is this only one person's impression or an impression shared by others?

(continued)

Giving Feedback

1. The receiver needs to be aware of what is being critiqued and what the measures are for judging it.

2. Feedback should be given as close to the time of the action or comment as possible. In that way, the receiver is most apt to be clear on exactly what is meant and can more easily recall the feelings of the action.

3. Feedback should be given when you think there is a good chance it will be accepted and deemed useful.

4. Feedback should be given only when there is an opportunity for change and/or improvement to occur.

5. Feedback should not be confused with, or used in place of, a demand or request for a change. Feedback says to the receiver, "Here's what I see happening. It's up to you to do what you will with my observation."

Receiving Feedback

1. Check what you have heard. Be sure you understand what the giver is trying to say. Because the topic is your own behavior, you may react prematurely and begin to think about what the feedback means before you are sure you are hearing the feedback as it is intended.

2. Don't be defensive. Feedback is neither right nor wrong. It is the reaction and feelings of the giver. Use your energy to hear and understand, not to defend and rebut.

Appendix:
Practice Negotiations

The New Financial Reporting System: DANA KENT

You are Dana Kent and your department needs a financial reporting system designed as soon as possible. You need to have the capability to do a number of things:

- track foreign currency fluctuations and their impact on cash flow;

- generate financial reports;

- do financial forecasting.

If possible, you also want the ability to present data graphically; this would greatly enhance the system.

You have a meeting scheduled with Lee Stone of IT to discuss both your needs and the assignment of someone to handle the job for you. You chatted with Lee briefly this morning and outlined your basic needs, although you didn't go into great detail.

The job must completed in no more than two months so that you can be ready for the new fiscal year which is three months away. However, your preference would be to finish the job in six weeks, which would give you the cushion you need to cover the problems that invariably happen on these jobs. You also want the time to train your staff and to run several tests of the system.

You would like Lee to assign Dale Clark, with whom you worked several years ago on a similar project. You know that Dale has the ability to turn out a top notch job within four to six weeks. In fact, you heard that he recently was promoted to supervisor.

You called Dale about this last week and he said that it sounded like an interesting assignment and, if the people "up top" agreed, he would have no objection to doing it.

You don't want IT to give you one of their new "hot shots," since you know they won't do half the job Dale will and would probably take a lot longer, going beyond your two month deadline. You don't want this job to be used as part of anyone's "on-the-job-training"—let them do that on a less important assignment. This assignment is critical and is a highly visible project.

You have enough in your budget to pay for this job, but since IT always wants to call all the shots, you feel that they should pay for the whole thing. You want to begin work immediately because this would get several people, including your boss, off your back. It will also ensure that your deadline is met, and send a message to everyone that work is underway.

You haven't had a great deal of contact with Lee but that which you have had has generally been positive.

The New Financial Reporting System: LEE STONE

You are Lee Stone, head of IT. Dana Kent of International Accounting called you this morning to discuss their need for a new financial reporting system. Dana didn't go into a great deal of detail, he only said that he would like to talk with you.

The design of this system doesn't sound difficult, in fact, it sounds like one that could be completed by one of your newer people in no more than two months. However, you'd like to get more time if you can—it would make life a lot easier. This assignment will provide the kind of exposure you want your new people to have and it will give them an opportunity to function as a consultant to another department. It is a good developmental assignment.

You have Elaine Stewart in mind for the assignment, although she couldn't begin for at least two weeks. Elaine has a good technical background as well as the type of people skills necessary to work with Accounting. You don't want to assign one of your more senior people to the job since it wouldn't be an effective use of your staff. Elaine has been at the company for about 8 months and has completed several assignments very successfully. Prior to joining the company she worked for a major bank, so she is very familiar with financial systems.

You believe that Dana may want Dale Clark to do this job, since Accounting was very pleased with the work he did several years ago on a similar project. However, Dale was promoted to a supervisory position about seven months ago and no longer designs this kind of system. However, he still reports to you.

You know the folks in Accounting. They're going to want you to cover a significant portion, if not all, of the cost of the job. Then they'll let everyone know how they got you to give them what they wanted. You'd like them to assume their fair share of the cost of the system, even though you could easily cover it. Like most people, they usually also overstate how quickly they need something done.

You haven't had a lot of contact with Dana, but that which you have had has always been positive.

THE ALPHA PROJECT: CHRIS

You (Chris) were very excited when your boss asked you to chair the Alpha Project team 18 months ago. You never chaired a team before and feel that this could have a positive impact on your career. The project involves the implementation of a new software program which could have a real bottom-line impact. Jim is one of the team members and you have worked on and off with him for the past several years. You generally find him responsive and easy to work with. However, he missed last month's meeting and just this morning called your secretary to say that he won't be available for next week's meeting. This is not typical. You're not happy with Jim's level of participation; you feel that he is ignoring his responsibilities to the team.

Namely:

- Jim has missed three meetings already. All in the last six months (and he hasn't sent anyone to cover for him). Prior to that time he was at every meeting.

- Jim's unavailability for meetings has resulted in the team being late with its monthly status reports on two separate occasions.

- Several weeks ago you had to make major revisions in Jim's section of the quarterly report because the piece he turned in was inadequate. If he had subnutted a draft of the report to you like everyone else, the problem could have been easily solved. This is not typical of Jim.

- Several times in the past three months you called ad-hoc meetings and weren't able to reach Jim. It would have been helpful if he'd been available, since these were issues he was knowledgeable about.

You can't afford to let Jim sacrifice your reputation. His performance (or lack thereof) is affecting the team. What makes the problem worse is that several team members have commented to you about Jim's performance and the effect it is having on the team. As one member said, "We need Data Coordination's input and if Jim can't participate, then we need someone who can."

You have spoken with your boss about the problem. She agreed with you as to the importance of the problem, but suggested that you try to work it out with Jim before she gets involved.

You really don't want your boss to intervene since it would indicate that you can't handle the tough problems. She did make it very clear that she is concerned and wants you to get the problem resolved —how is up to you. Both of you see this project as critical.

You have asked to meet with Jim in an effort to let him know how you feel and to see if these problems can be solved and put behind you. You have not talked to Jim about your concerns before today.

Known to Both Parties

You chair the Alpha project team. Jim represents Data Coordination. Both of you are at the same organizational level.

THE ALPHA PROJECT: JIM

You (Jim) and Chris have been working on the Alpha Project team for the past 18 months. You represent Data Coordination.

You and Chris are at the same organizational level; Chris was asked to head up the project team. While you generally like Chris and have enjoyed working with her in the past, you think her appointment was a mistake. A number of people, yourself included, would have been better choices. This project involves the implementation of a new software program that could have a significant impact on the company.

You are not happy with the way Chris has treated you on this project.

Namely:

- She has made several major changes in your section of the quarterly report without asking for or getting your approval. You were away on a trip, but she could have gotten to you with a little effort.

- Chris has been meeting informally with other members of the team and for some reason never invites you.

- She has put you on the spot at several meetings by asking you to respond to questions you were not prepared to discuss.

You've also heard through the grapevine that Chris feels you were responsible for the team being late with its monthly reports. She never even talked about this with you!

Chris has asked to meet with you—probably because you missed the last meeting because of a field visit. In addition, you had your secretary call to say you may have to miss next week's meeting because of another trip. his is not the first meeting you have missed and since you were recently assigned to a second project team, you will mostly likely miss others. In the past six months you have missed three meetings. In fact, because you are short staffed, you haven't even sent people to cover for you.

This is not an easy problem. Chris behaves as if Data Coordination has nothing to do but wait for this project. Your department is short-staffed. Several people recently retired and were not replaced. As a result, your boss has gotten you involved in several other projects. As he said to you recently, "We need you to cover at least two other teams where they need our input. Do what you have to keep on top of the Alpha Project, but don't let these other projects slip." When you mentioned the importance of the Alpha Project, he indicated that he thought its potential was being overrated and said, "... anyway, we have no choice. We just have to do the best we can." This whole thing really bothers you. You don't want this project or Chris to fail, but yet you don't see any real options. You are glad Chris asked to meet, since you have wanted to get these issues settled.

Known to Both Parties

Chris chairs the Alpha project team. You represent Data Coordination. Both of you are at the same organizational level.

INDEX